# Carving Mountain Men

## with Cleve Taylor

Text written with and photography by Jeffrey B. Snyder

4880 Lower Valley Road, Atglen, PA 19310 USA

## Dedication

As always in everything I do, to Sandy with love and thanks for the good life we have together.

## Contents

Introduction  4

Carving the Mountain Man  5

Painting the Mountain Man  50

Patterns  58

Gallery  62

Copyright © 1998 by Cleve Taylor
Library of Congress Catalog Card Number: 98-85389

All rights reserved. No part of this work may be reproduced or used in any form or by any means—graphic, electronic, or mechanical, including photocopying or information storage and retrieval systems—without written permission from the copyright holder.

"Schiffer," "Schiffer Publishing Ltd. & Design," and the "Design of pen and ink well" are registered trademarks of Schiffer Publishing, Ltd.

This book is meant only for personal home use and recreation. It is not intended for commercial applications or manufacturing purposes.

Designed by Laurie A. Smucker
Typeset in Zapf Humanist 601 BT

ISBN: 0-7643-0654-5
Printed in China

Published by Schiffer Publishing Ltd.
4880 Lower Valley Road
Atglen, PA 19310
Phone: (610) 593-1777; Fax: (610) 593-2002
Please write for a free catalog.
This book may be purchased from the publisher.
Please include $3.95 for shipping.

In Europe, Schiffer books are distributed by
Bushwood Books
6 Marksbury Avenue
Kew Gardens
Surrey TW9 4JF England
Phone: 44 (0)181 392-8585; Fax: 44 (0)181 392-9876
e-mail: bushwd@aol.com

Try your bookstore first.

We are interested in hearing from authors with book ideas on related subjects.

# Introduction

The inspirations for this book came from two friends of mine who live and work in Hailey, Idaho, just a stones throw from the famous Sun Valley Resort. John Davies is a mountain man. Well, at least, a couple times a years he dons his buckskins, head dress, possibles bag, powder horn, moccasins, and musket to join several hundred others like himself at a rendezvous for mountain men and their women. John's wife, Joan Davies (alias Shining Moon), dresses in her white buckskin dress and energetically plays her role as her mountain man's woman.

Joan asked me several years ago to carve a likeness of John in his mountain man dress and supplied me with a photograph of John all decked out. Time passed and several years later I got around to carving the old coot. Before I could deliver the finished piece to Joan, I had an opportunity to show it off at several gatherings for wood-carvers. Amber Hahn of Yakima, Washington, saw it and commenced to add it to her collection. Well, I had to carve another one for Joan, but Richard Rose saw it and became the new owner. So, I had to carve a third for Joan. An anonymous client had to have that one and then Larry Crist had to have the next one for his collection. When folks in Vancouver saw Larry's, *they* wanted a class, and so on and so forth. Meanwhile, my old outmoded computer between my ears started whirring, clinking and clanking, and I had an idea! Since this fellow is so popular, why not do a project book on the old boy. I suppose it is kind of obvious by now that I did ... write a book on the mountain man that is.

When I arrived at Schiffer Publishing for the photography shoot, I was delighted to find Tom Wolfe doing a shoot just a few feet from my work station. If by chance you see any similarity between my mountain man and Tom, it is purely coincidental. However, his hairy face and North Carolina aura had to have influenced my carving. Tom, his lovely wife Nancy, and I spent a week together in Atglen, Pennsylvania, and I enjoyed every minute of the time. Thanks Tom and Nancy and John and Joan Davies, I hope you enjoy this book as much as I have.

As an ending to this story, Joan finally got the carving of her mountain man. She gave it to John for his birthday and wrote a beautiful story called *A Gift of Two Diamonds* to accompany the carving. I have asked for her permission to print this story and I am including it with this introduction.

## A Gift of Two Diamonds—
## With Love by Shining Moon

A large bang echoed above the canyon walls. Everyone froze in silence wondering the origin of the noise. It wasn't long until a large full figured man appeared on the horizon and started to descend the steep terrain. The moonlight reflected off the top of a red fur hat. He was clothed in leather buckskins with fringe that swayed as he approached our evening campfire. As he moved closer, you could see the color of his hat blended with the color of his hair and beard.

His loud booming voice was now echoing with excitement as he approached our campfire. "Howdy folks, how are you doing this fine evening." Our fear left us as we saw his smiling face in the campfire light. The butt of his old 54 caliber muzzle loader gun glistened as he moved the gun to a secure resting spot near a large rock. The patchbox was engraved with a running bear. That must have been the object that swiped the silence of the evening.

We returned his greeting and invited him to join the circle. Everyone got comfortable round the crackling fire. The smell of sage smoke penetrated the evening air. It wasn't long before the conversation turned to some little short tales and then they became longer and taller. It was becoming a contest to see who could outwit the other tellers. Our new guest let us know he had two names. One was Running Bear and the other was Big John.

Running Bear was the name he received from Indians after he encountered, outwitted, and out ran a large grizzly bear on an adventure through the Rockies. None of us were sure he could have ever survived such an event. But there he sat as big as could be. Big John was given to him by other mountain men who trapped beaver in the Sawtooths.

His stories continued and for some strange reason our interest stayed peaked—particularly when he started talking about the time he traveled into the Snake River country. He found a great spring of crystal clear water flowing from the rock walls. Of course he was very thirsty and drank his fill of the cool liquid.

He later found a comfortable soft spot on the ground, laid down, and was soon in dream land. His dream took him to a time many years ago when the river was very narrow and could be crossed by walking from bank to bank. A time before the big dams were built. He told us he would never have believed that there were enough beavers to build dams as big as the lakes now on the river. A time when antelope, deer, and buffalo roamed free and the beaver were plentiful. He was able to bring in a large supply of pelts to the fall rendezvous near the hot springs under the mighty Tetons. The rendezvous was a fun spot to see old friends, refresh his supplies and acquire numerous treasures for Indian friends in the mountains to the west.

Years ago, an old Shoshoni woman beaded him a neckpiece to protect his skin from the sun. She used brain tanned deerskin leather to support the beads she had traded for the year before. In the center of the tie she placed two diamonds, symbols of this man's two patterns of life. Each contained a red center. The top one was surrounded with the white and a blue geometric border, the bottom was surrounded with bright yellow and a feathered blue border. On the back she used a floral rose piece of fabric that once was a piece of a cotton shirt she found along a trail. The skirt had been left behind by someone on a wagon train. Big John was showing the prized piece to a young Indian boy who showed much interest in the work. He recognized the rose floral fabric. It was made from the skirt his grandmother had. The Indian boy knew he could respect this man. He had always trusted the judgement of his grandmother. She only created her beadwork for those she trusted, liked, and understood. Big John took the piece from his neck and handed it to the young boy to examine. Tears welled in both of their eyes as the boy told Big John of his grandmother's death in the early spring. The news saddened Big John and he sat and reminisced with the boy of fond stories of the life of an Indian woman named "Spring Rain." Yes, she died in the spring when the grass was green from the spring rain and it left a promise of a good summer. Both felt better sharing stories of a gentle woman famous for great beadwork.

Big John knew he should find a special gift for his new young friend at the rendezvous. Something that would remind him of his grandmother who saw the best in people and interpreted it in her beadwork. Something that would never let him forget her quality of understanding people. His dream ended looking for this special gift. His first waking thoughts were to continue his search.

As the story unfolded, he was asking us to join his search and look for the perfect gift for his friend. We liked this man of large stature who valued kindness, gentleness, and returned favors. We each wanted to help in the search. On his side hung a large bag and we all wondered what other treasures were in his purse. We asked the question. He said, "Well almost anything that is possible could be in this here possibles bag." Everyone still wondered what was really contained within but all just laughed at the comment. How many more tall tales could he tell that would make us wonder if they were true or did we discover the truth that came from his myth. This man was large and bold but gentle and kind. The neckpiece of two diamonds, the diamonds with different borders—the sharp geometric shape represented the large and bold, the soft feathered border represented the gentle and kind side. Spring Rain beaded us a treasure. We recognized the gift by understanding the person. That's the perfect gift for the boy. The grandmother's message would always remain with her grandson. A gift he could keep forever—the gift of understanding.

## Tools

Here are the tools you will need for this project:

I use a Kevlar carving glove impervious to knife cuts, a series of bench knives, a Foredom or Dremel rotary power tool with a Kutzall burr, and a band saw. The gouges I use are a 1/4" #9 gouge, 1/2" #3 fishtail gouge, three different size V tools (1/4", 1/8", and a micro 2mm or 1/16" V gouge), a 3/16" deep gouge, a 1/8" #5, and a 1/2" #7 gouge, and a 3/32" deep gouge (deep gouges are also called veiners).

# Carving the Mountain Man

Are you ready to carve this mountain man?

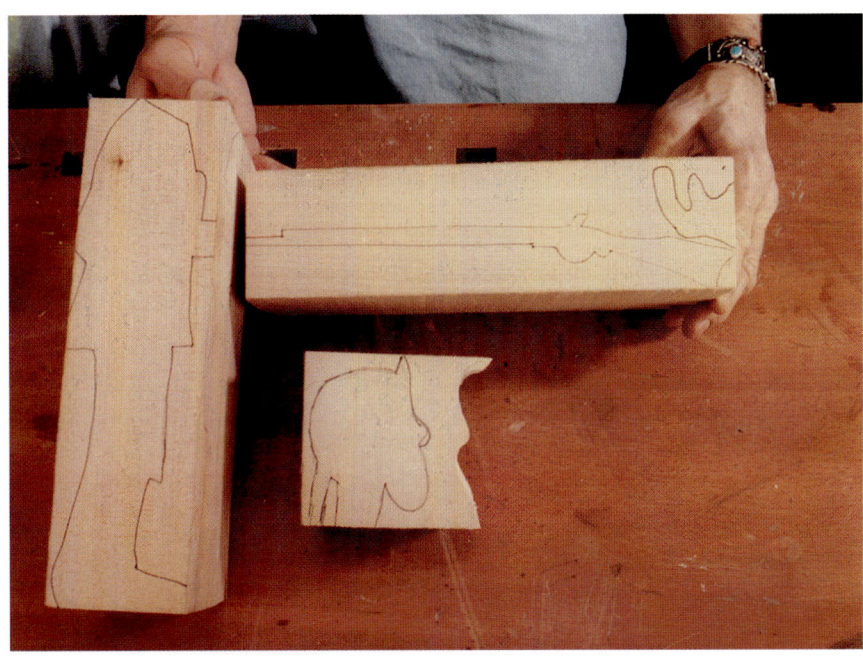

Transfer the pattern for the mountain man and his rifle to your basswood blocks. The body is carved from a piece of wood measuring 3" thick x 5" wide x 11" long. The head pattern is on a 3" x 3" x 4" long block. The rifle and hands are carved from a basswood block that is 3" wide x 11" long x 2" thick.

Using a band saw, follow the pattern lines to cut away excess wood and create your carving blanks for the head, body, hands, and rifle. Once we have cut out the profile view of the body, we will cut out the front view shown here. The neck hole is drilled using a 1" diameter drill bit.

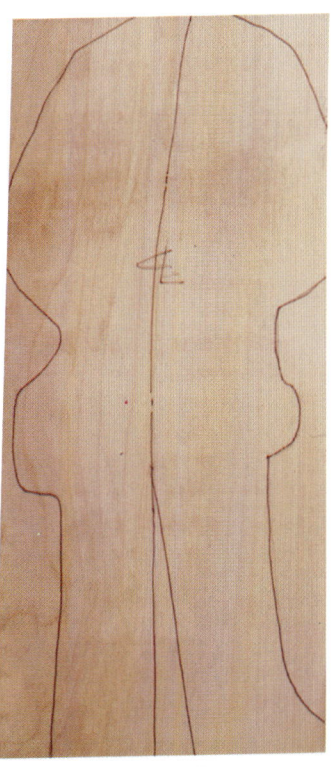

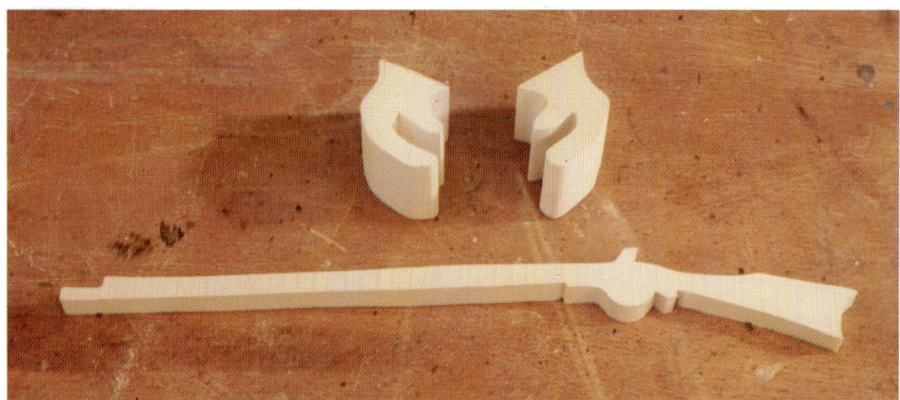

The two hands are cut from a single pattern drawn on a 2" thick board. Cutting the board into two equal halves gives you two hands from this single pattern. The rifle is cut 1/2" thick.

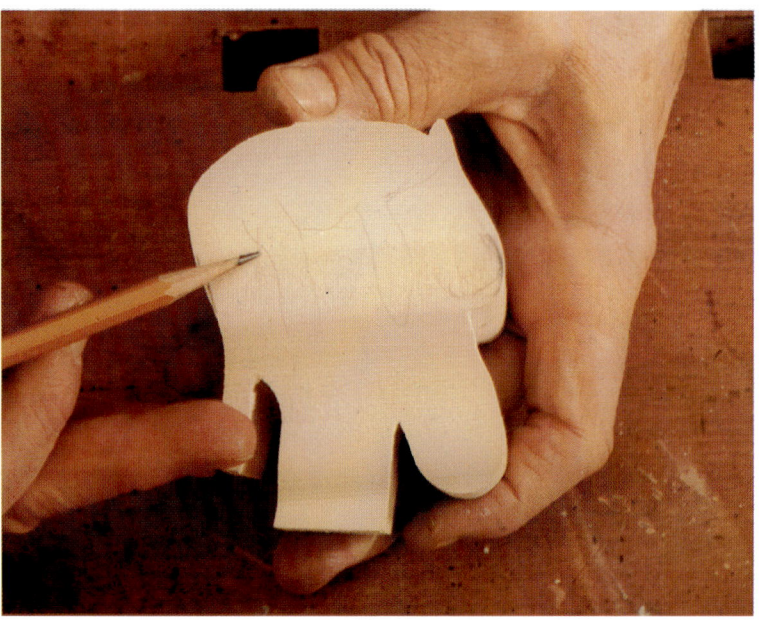

Here is the profile of the head with the legs and body of the hat sketched on.

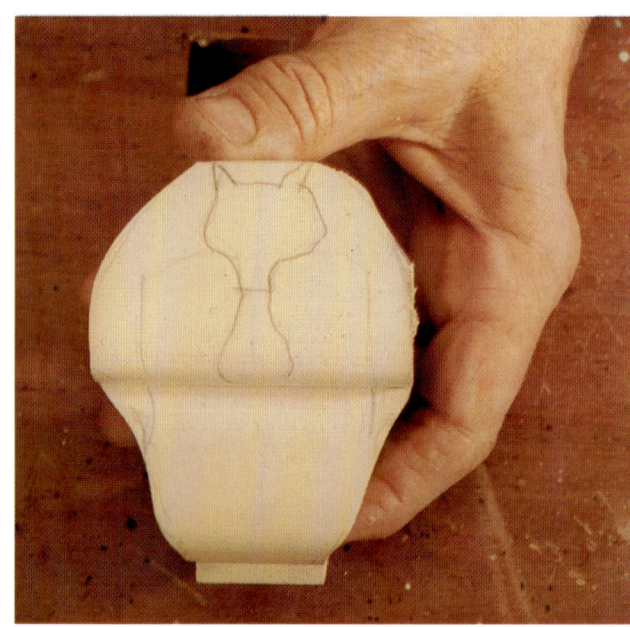

This is the front of the head, with sketches of the animal's head and mountain man's nose drawn on.

Using a Kutzall Burr in a Foredom machine, remove excess wood from the head.

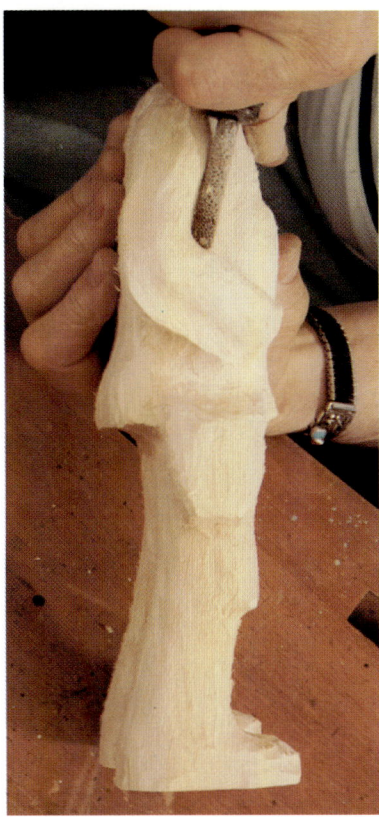

Here is the side view of the body after removing the excess wood with the Foredom equipped with the Kutzall Burr.

This is the front view of the body after the excess wood has been removed ... again with the Kutzall Burr.

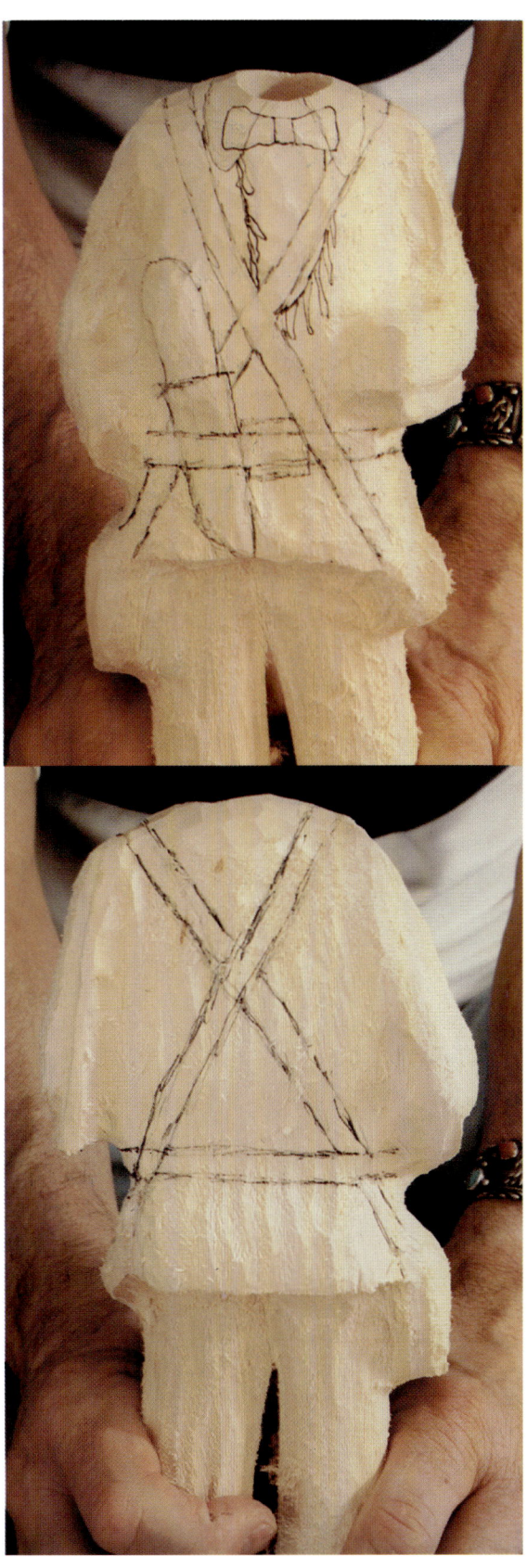

On the torso, draw in the details of the knife, belt, straps, the chest opening in the shirt, and the collar.

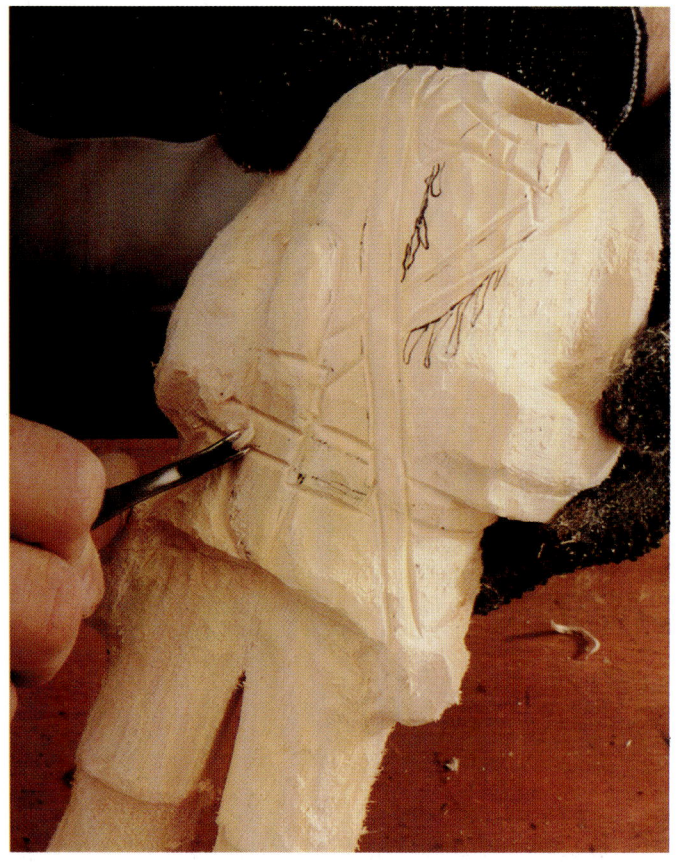

Use a large V tool to outline the knife, straps, belt, and collar.

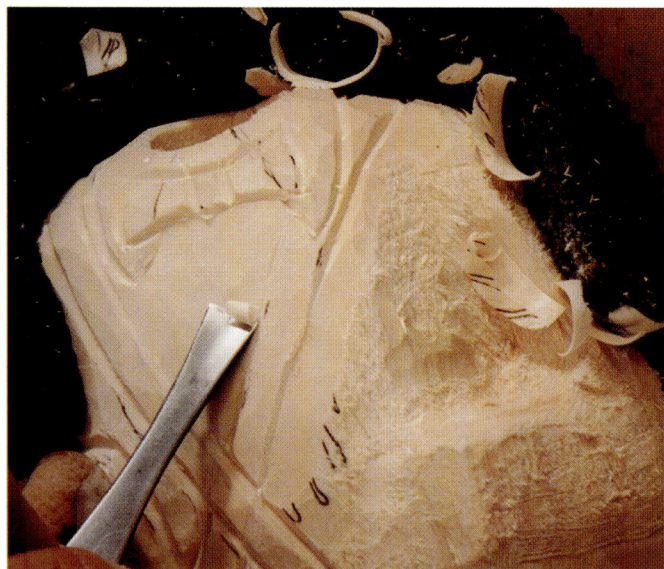

Relieve the area of the shirt opening between the straps and under the collar.

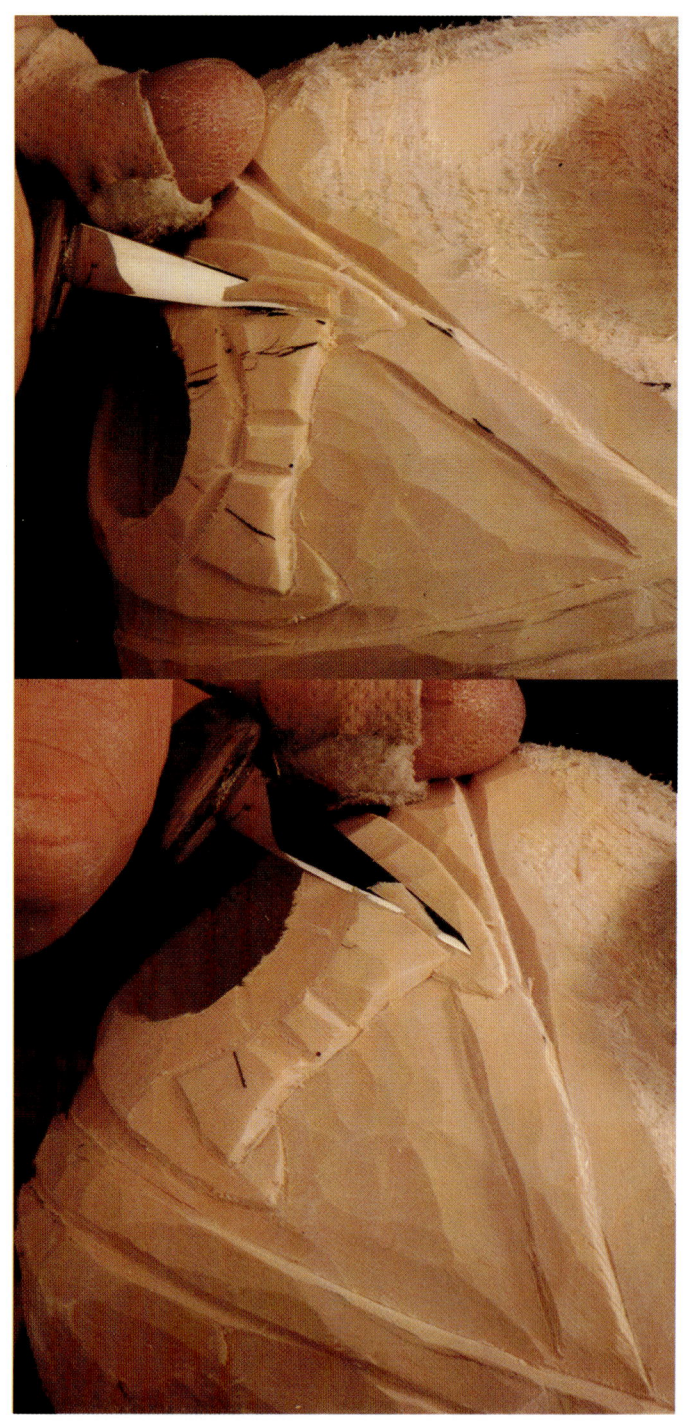

Use your knife and/or flat gouges to relieve the collar of the buckskin shirt to the reeded portion of the beaded breast plate (see the completed carving for details).

Sketch in the area of the beaded breast plate. It will be behind the opening in the buckskin shirt. The edge of the shirt is fringed.

Draw in the breast plate's beadwork and its reeds between the collars.

Relieve the breast plate area to a depth of about 1/16" below the outside surface of the buckskin shirt. Place in a few V cuts along the left hand side where fringe overlaps the breast plate.

You might want to strop your small V tool before proceeding with the next step. Otherwise, you are going to make hash out of the beadwork.

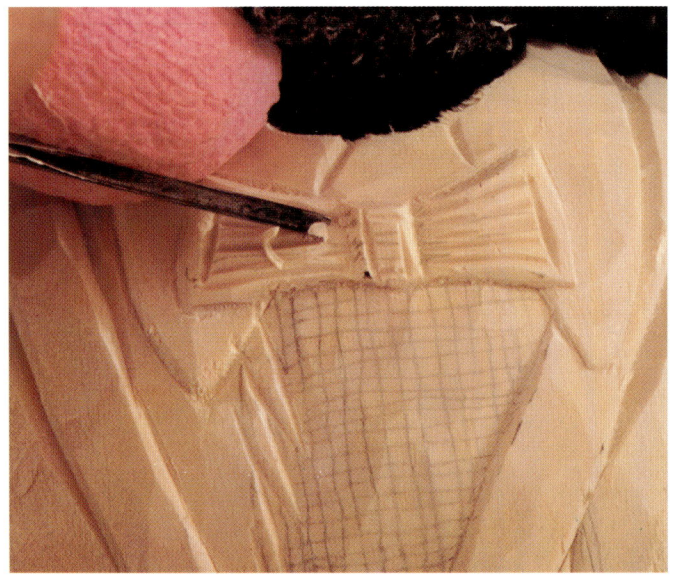

First carve in the reeds as drawn.

Carve in the horizontal lines.

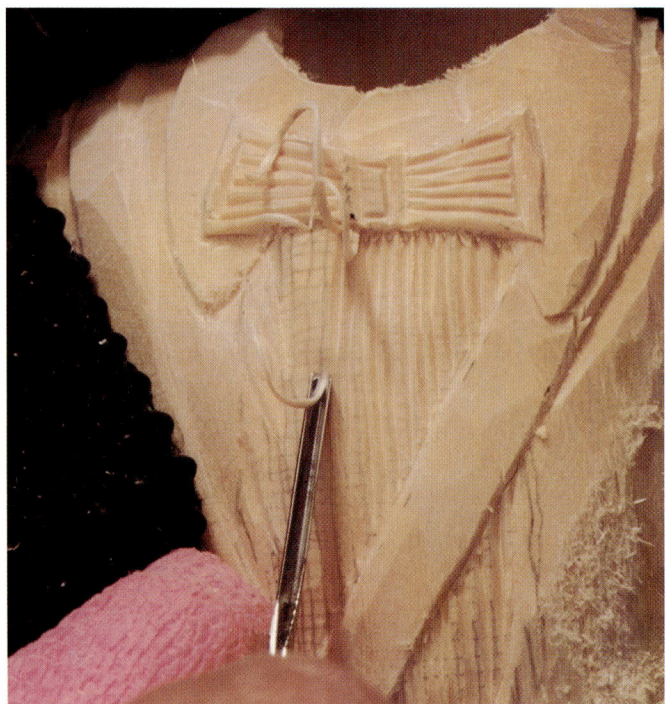

Carve in the vertical lines of the beadwork.

The carving on the beadwork is completed. If you have made your cuts very clean in this area, painting will enhance the definition of the beads later on.

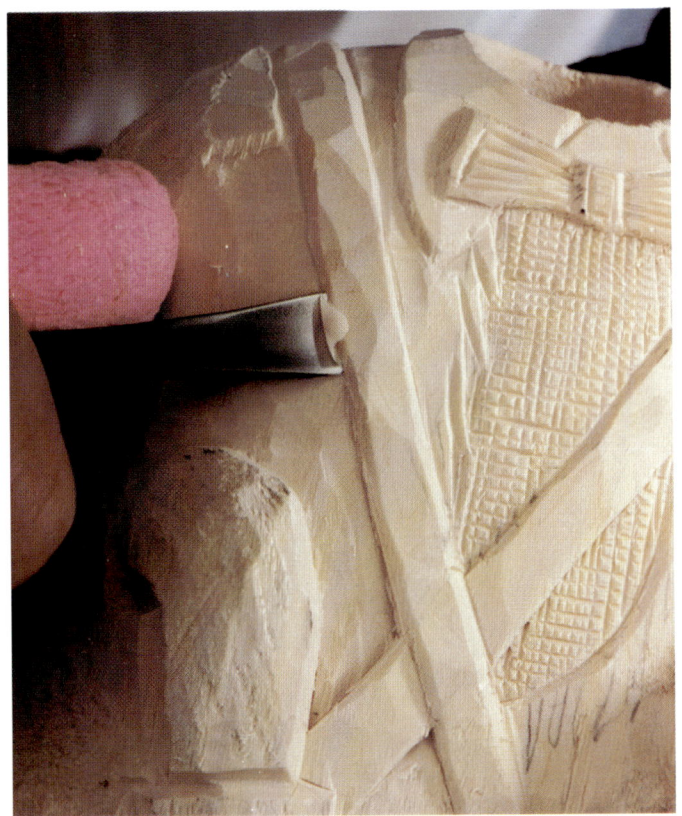

Continue to relieve the buckskin shirt around the straps and the knife

The knife handle is relieved with a detail knife.

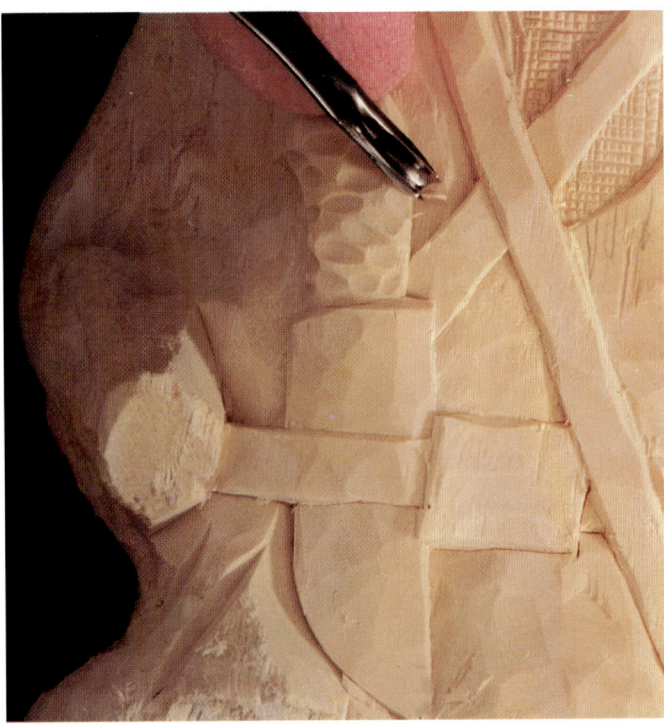

Use a 1/8" deep gouge and cut in the handle of the knife with short strokes to simulate bone.

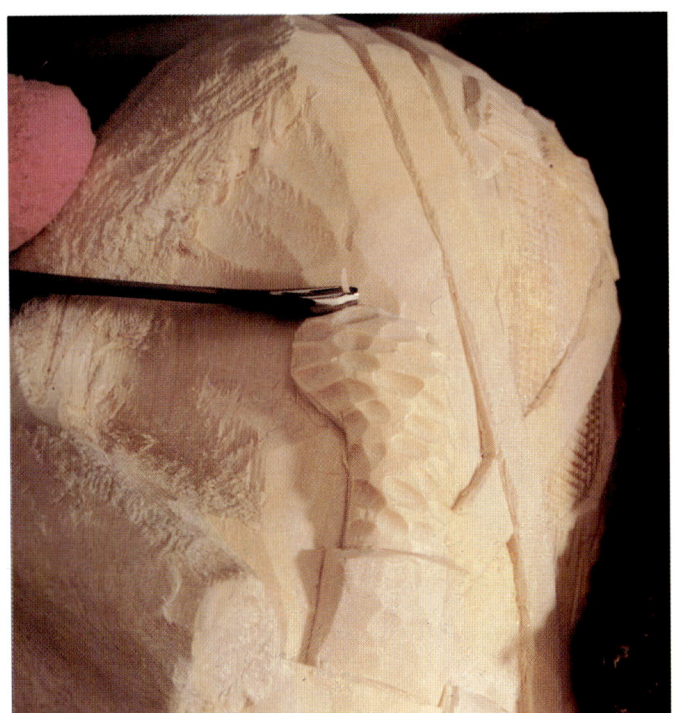

Like so.

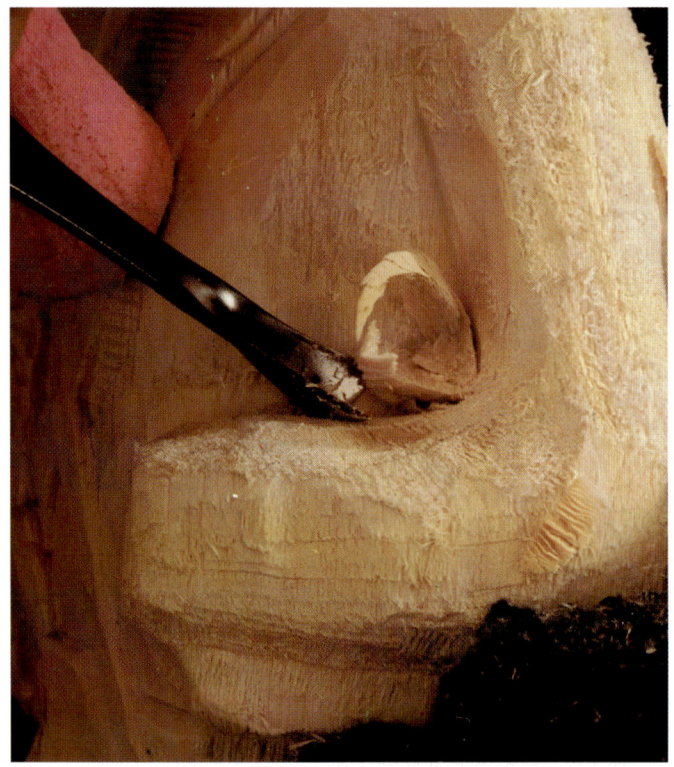

Using a large V tool, separate the arm from the body.

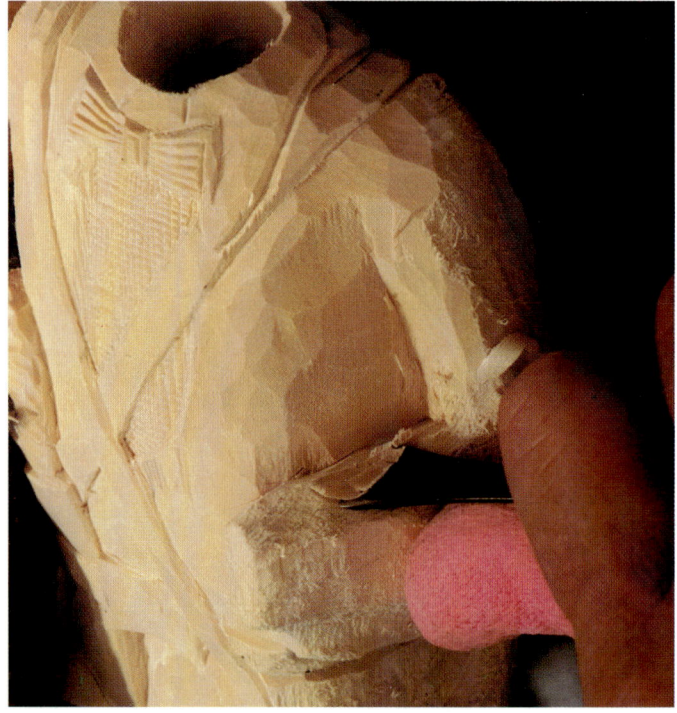

and the arm to the body.

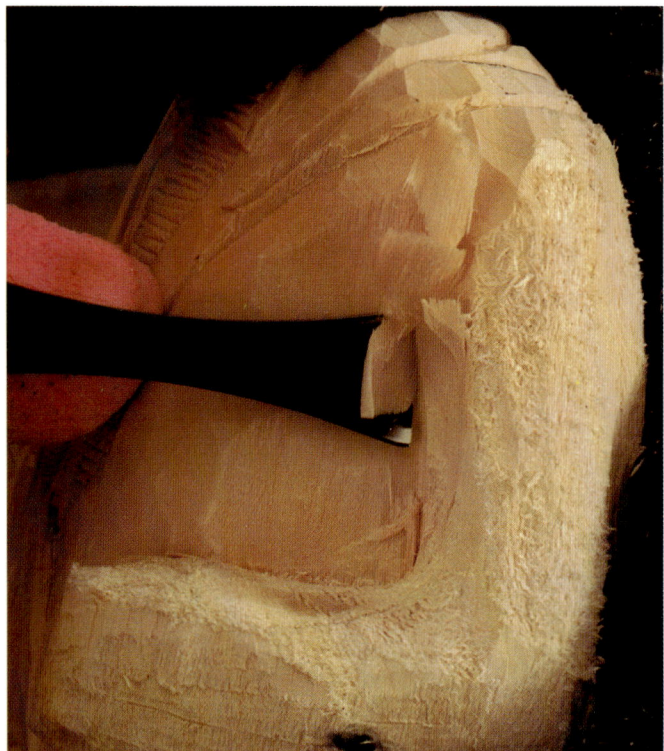

With a large, 3/4" wide fishtail gouge, begin to relieve the body to the arm ...

This is the result of relieving the body to the arm and the arm to the body.

Separate both the wrist and the fringe along the bottom of the sleeve from the body.

Use the large V tool to outline the powder horn.

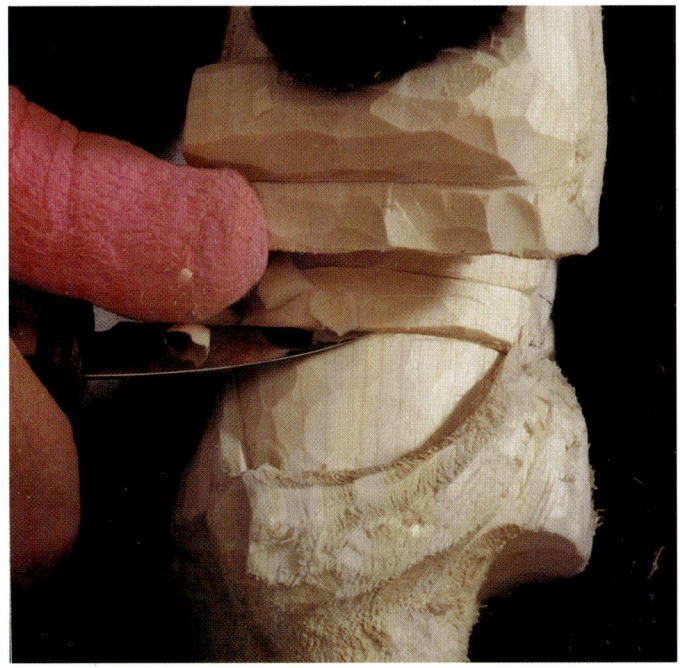

Begin to relieve between the bottom of the belt and the top of the powder horn.

Use gouges to clean burr marks and saw marks from the powder horn.

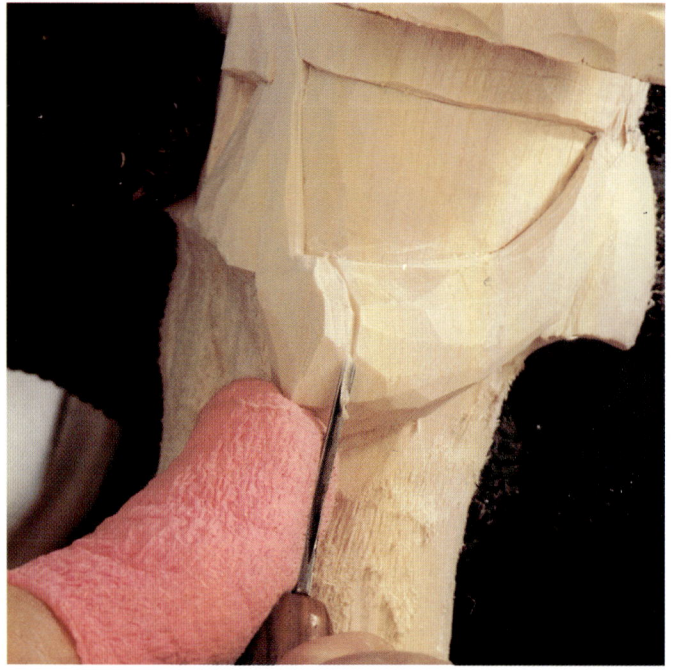

Cut in the leather cap that covers the end of the powder horn.

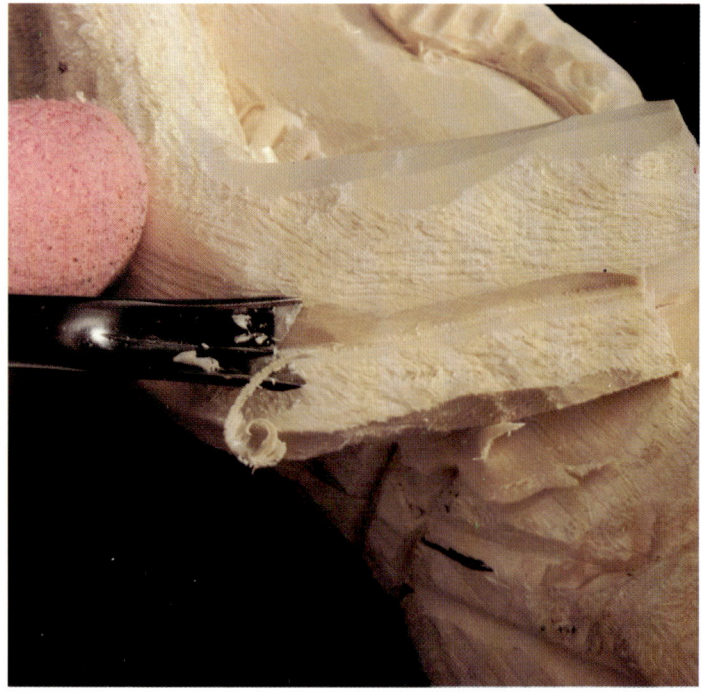

Using a large V tool, separate the fringe on the shirt sleeve from the coat.

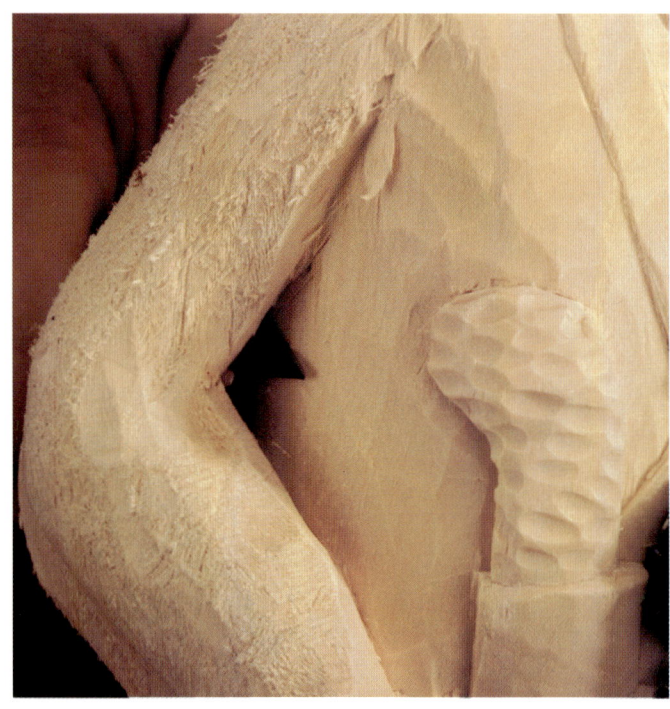

Begin to show some space between the crook of the right arm and the body.

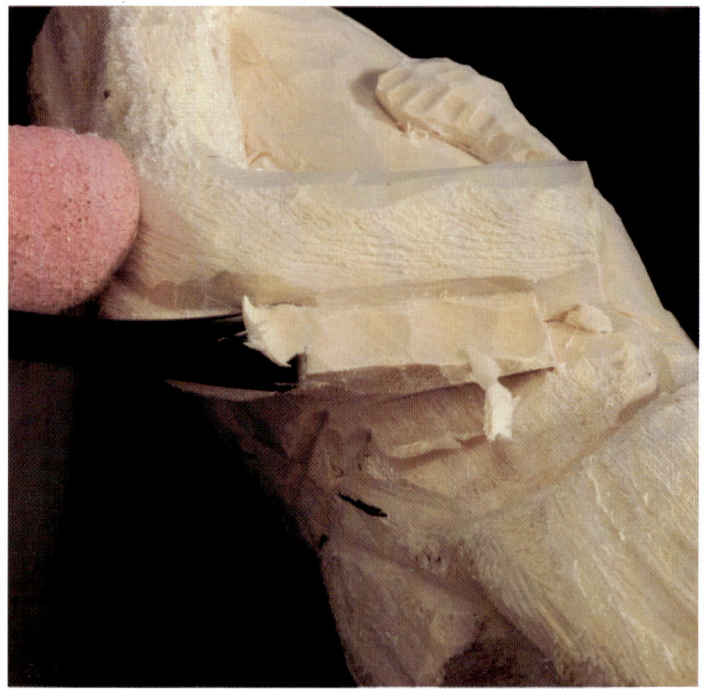

Clean the burr marks and texture the fringe using a large, shallow gouge.

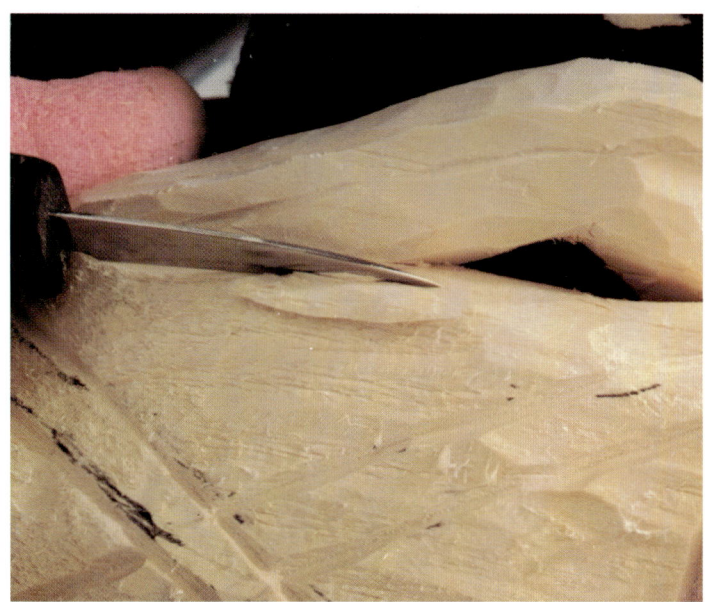

A hole is now cut between the right arm and body. The arm has been rounded and smoothed and the shirt fringe mound is separated and defined, ready for the fringe detail.

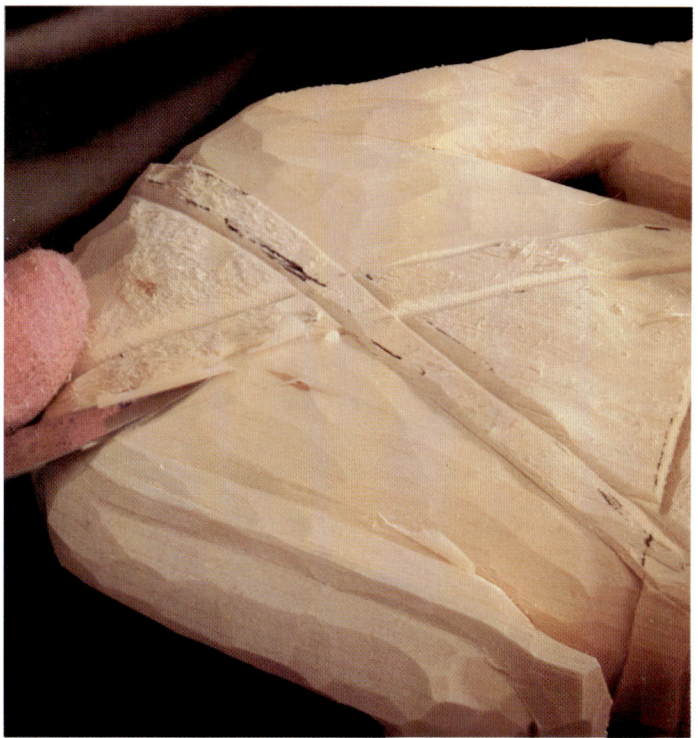

Continue to relieve the buckskin shirt between straps.

Begin to relieve wood from between the underside of the right arm and the top of the "possibles" bag.

I use this large, 3/4" wide fishtail gouge for relief work on large surfaces.

After the relief work is done on the buckskin shirt, use a flat gouge to clean off the straps.

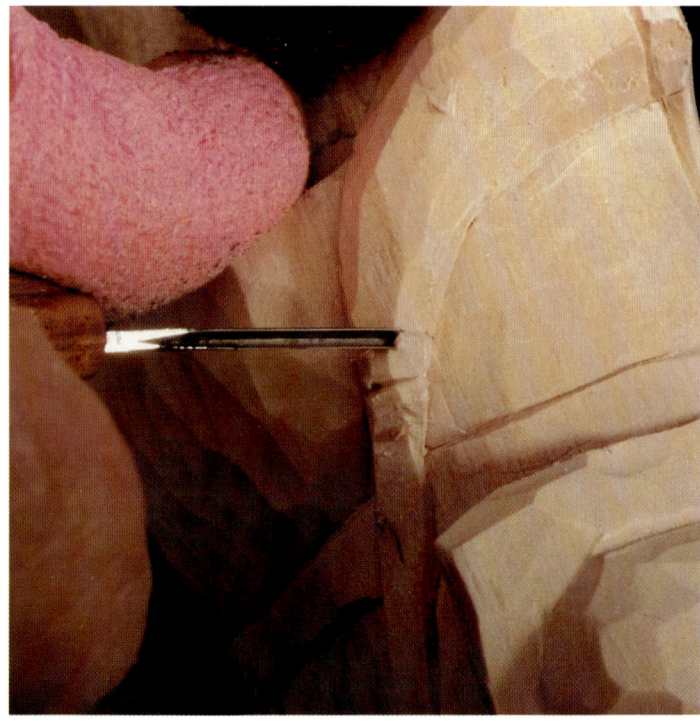

Use your small V to carve in the cap at the small end of the powder horn.

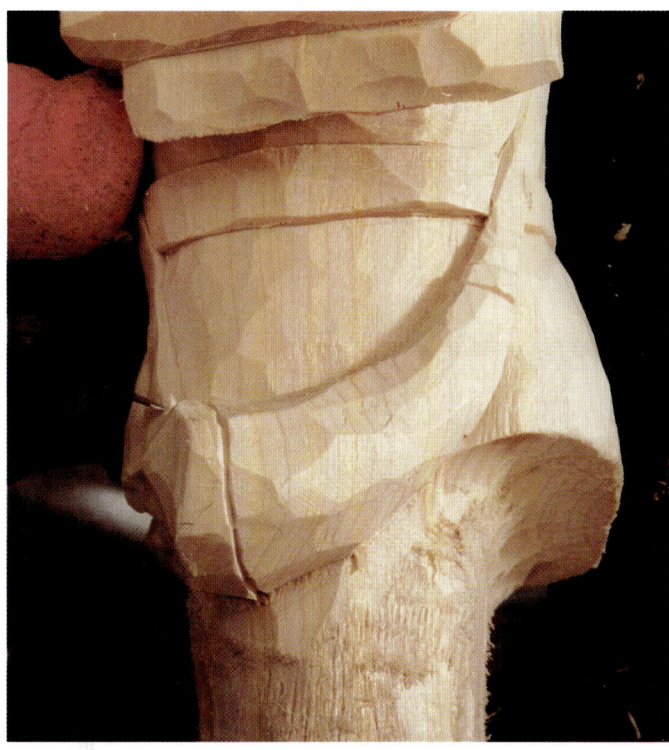

Both the powder horn and the area adjacent to it are complete.

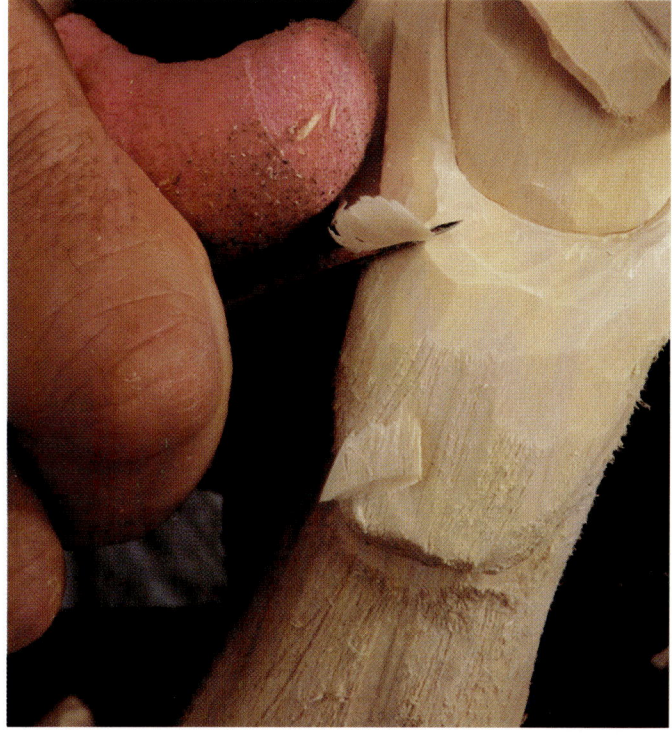

Use a knife and/or flat gouge to clean the burr and saw marks from the surface of the possibles bag.

Begin work on the possibles bag, separating it from the pant leg with a large V tool.

Use your knife tip to deepen the separation between the leg and the bag.

17

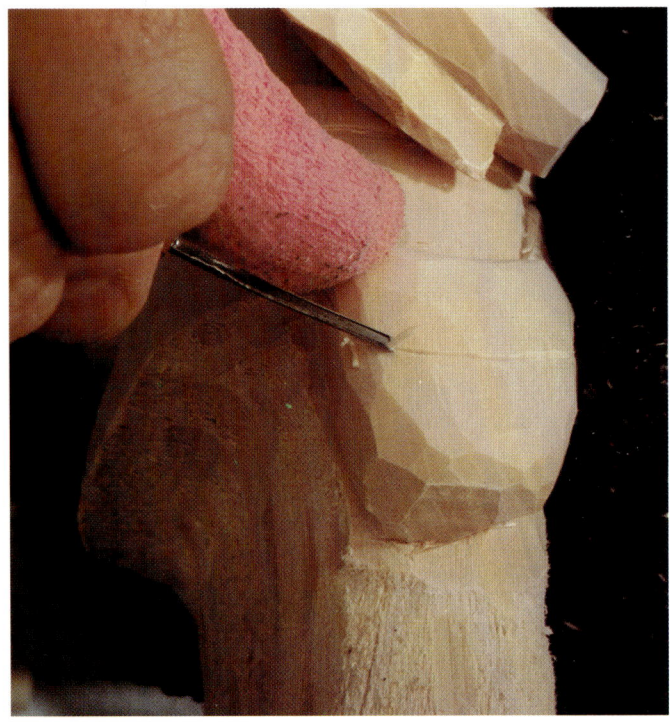

Use a small V tool to outline the cover flap of the bag.

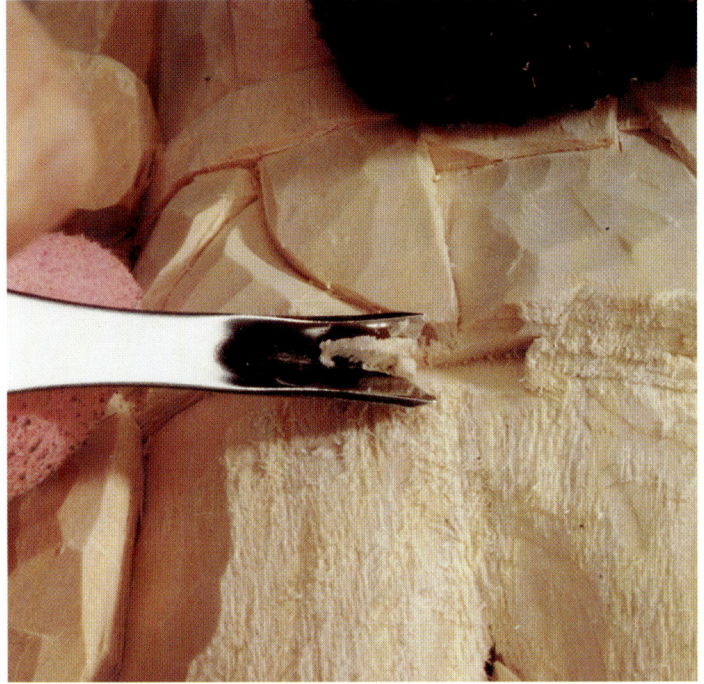

Use your large V tool to separate the bottom of the buckskin shirt from the pants.

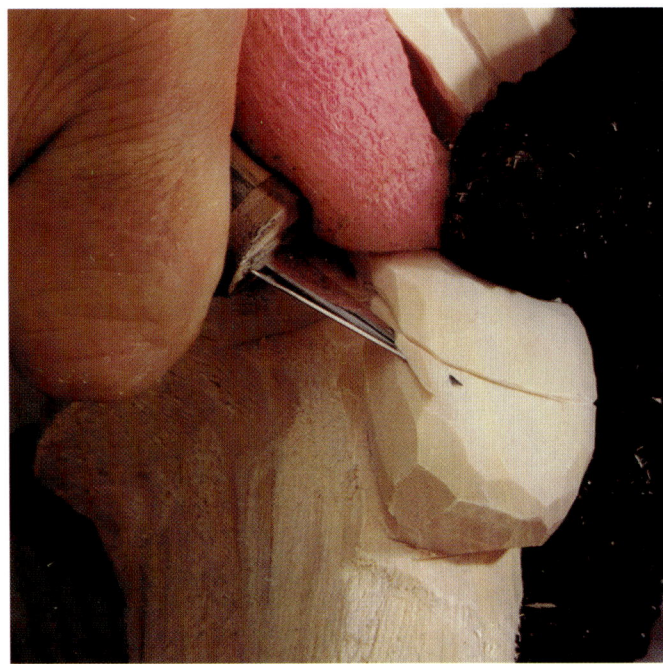

Use your knife to relieve the bag below the flap.

Lay in your knife flat along the leg and extend the line of the leg up under the buckskin shirt.

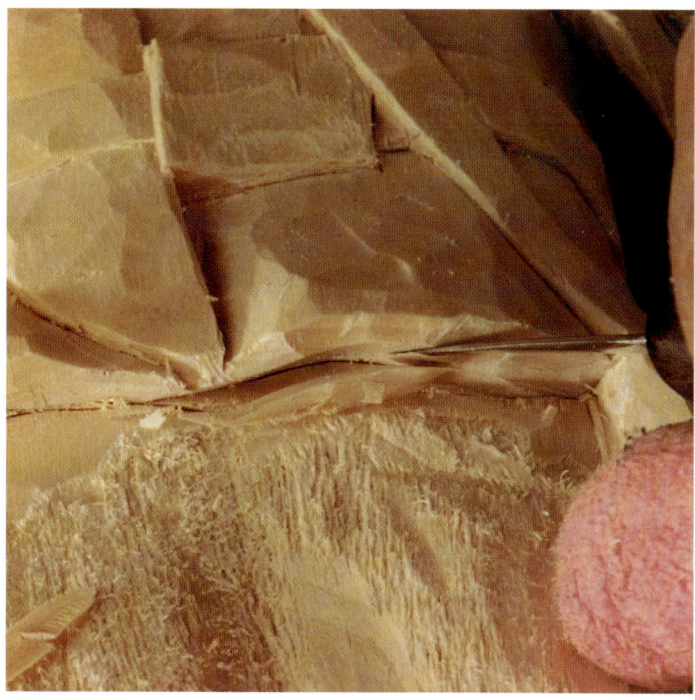

At an angle of about 45 degrees to the pant leg, undercut the shirt.

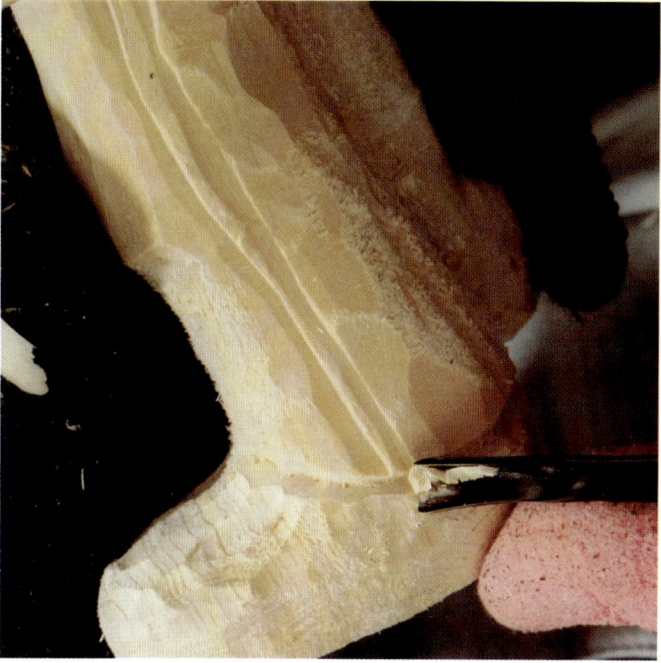

Here we have cut in the bottom of the buckskin pant leg and we have also created a slim mound along the outside of the pant leg onto which we will carve fringe.

The undercut along the front of the buckskin shirt is complete.

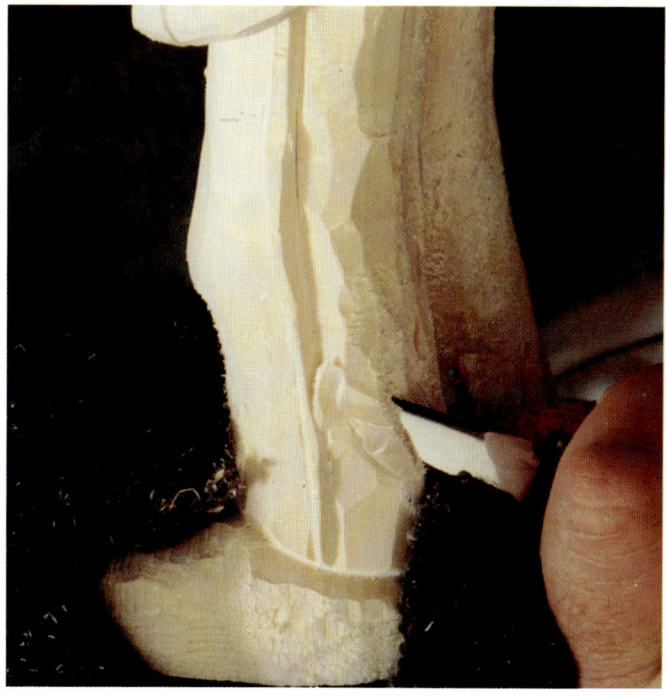

Relieve the leg, leaving the mound for the fringe raised above the surface of the pant leg.

19

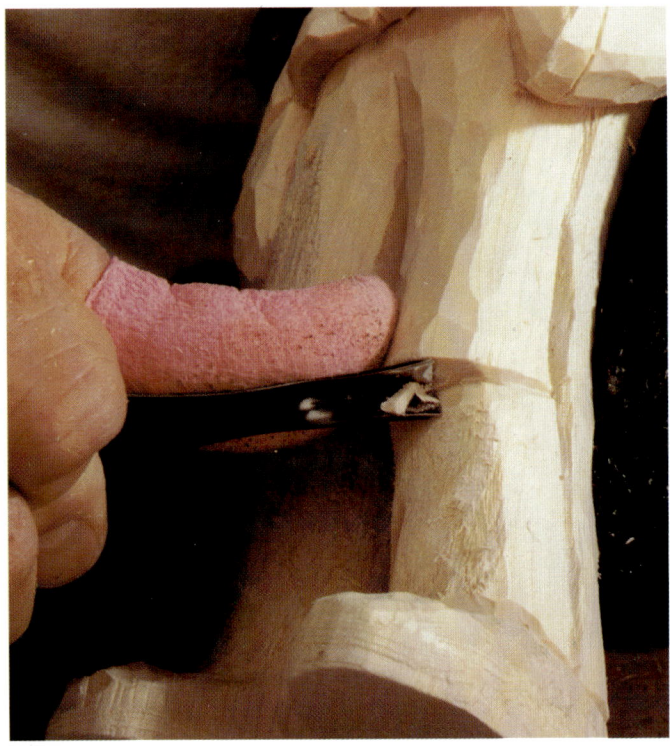

Use your V tool to carve the underside of the fringe located along the knee flap.

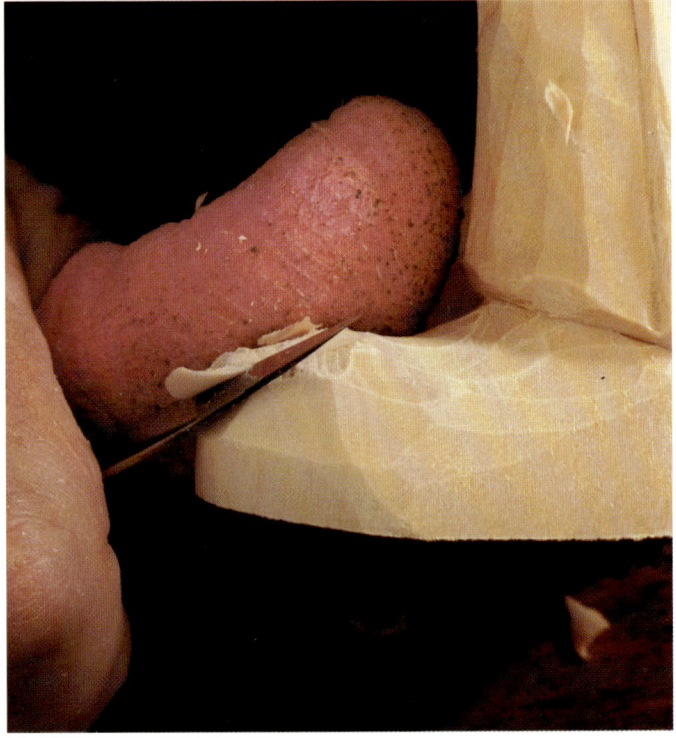

Use your knife to shape the moccasin.

Use your knife to relieve the moccasin underneath the pant leg.

Use your knife to scoop out the underside of the moccasin a bit to show a very slight heel.

Draw a line as shown around the top of the moccasin. We will cut this in as a seam line. The upper surface of the moccasin will feature beadwork similar to the breast plate.

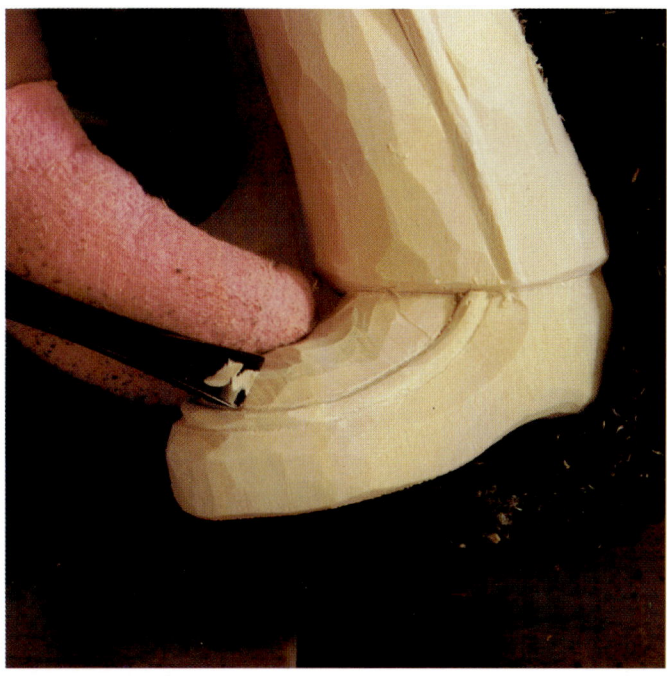

Relieving the moccasin.

Use a V tool to form the mound of the seam line. Use knives and gouges to relieve the moccasin to the depth of the V cut around this mound.

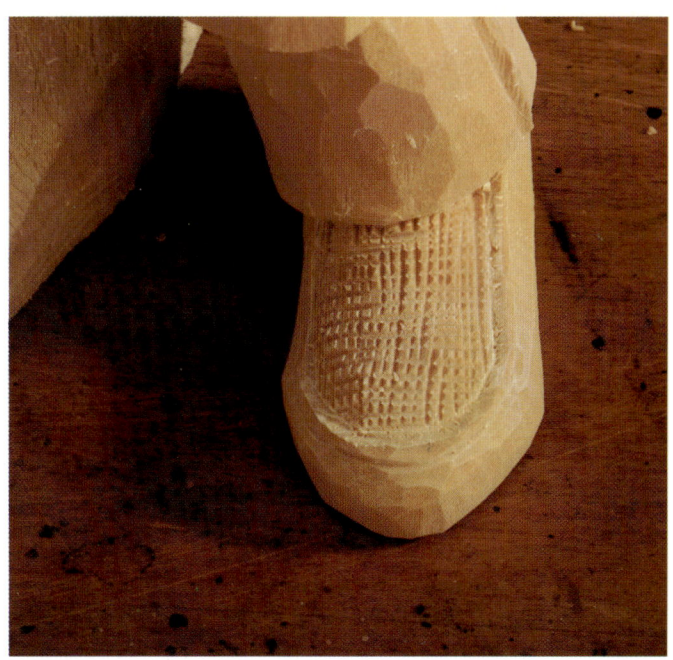

Beadwork has been applied to the top of the moccasin in the same manner as on the breast plate. Remember to make sure that small V tool is sharp!

Let's undercut the fringe at the knee now.

Before we start detailing the fringe on the buckskin shirt and pants, let's construct some wrinkles around the elbow and upper arm. Generally the wrinkles in these two areas will follow the flow I've penciled in here.

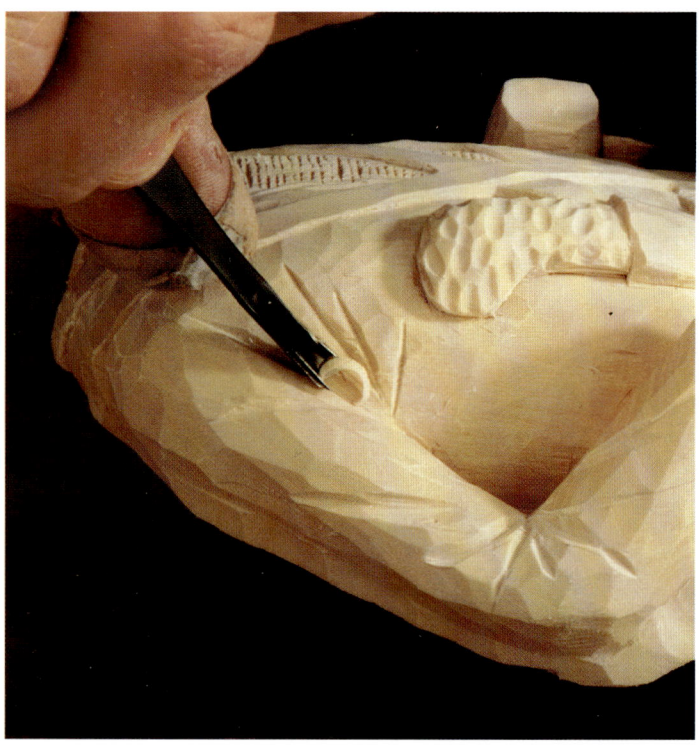

In carving these wrinkles, I generally begin by using a large V tool and cutting fairly deeply along the flow lines.

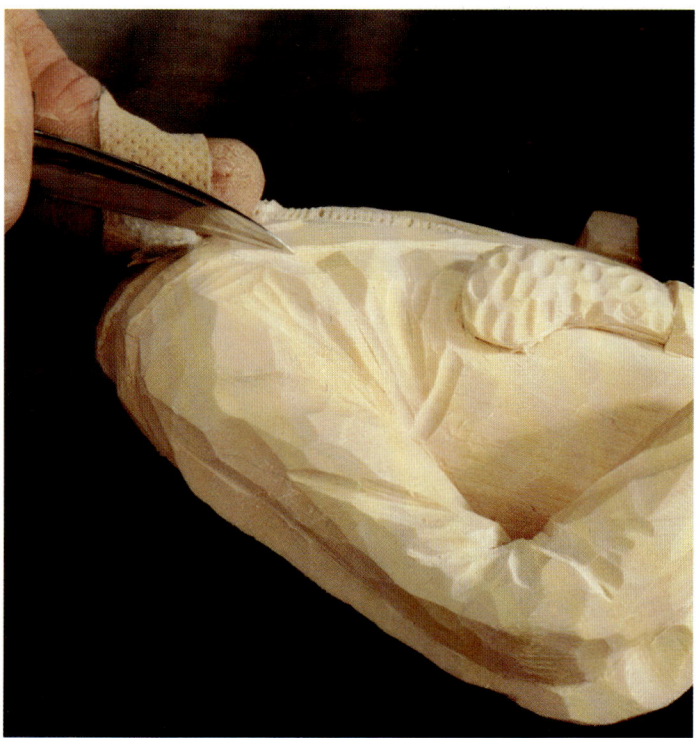

Use a large, deep gouge such as the 1/4" #9 to broaden, deepen, and (in some cases) completely obliterate the V cuts of the wrinkles.

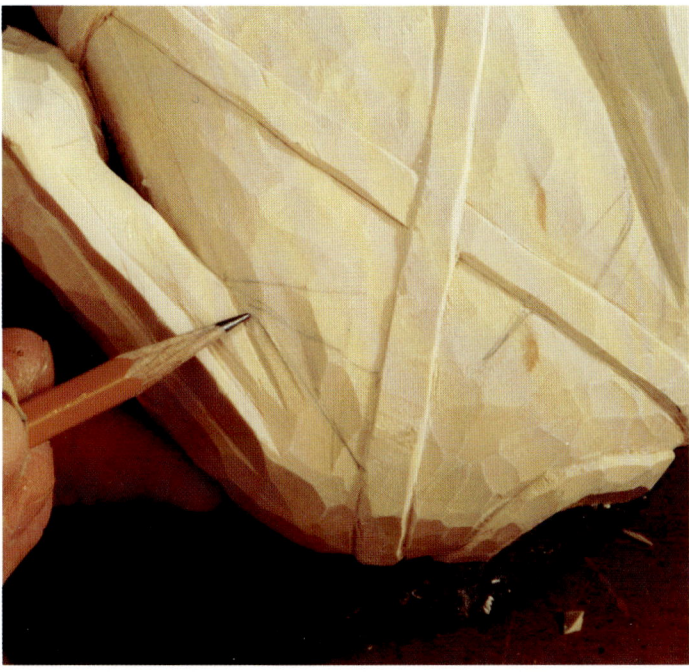

Draw in the flow of the wrinkles on the back of the shirt as well.

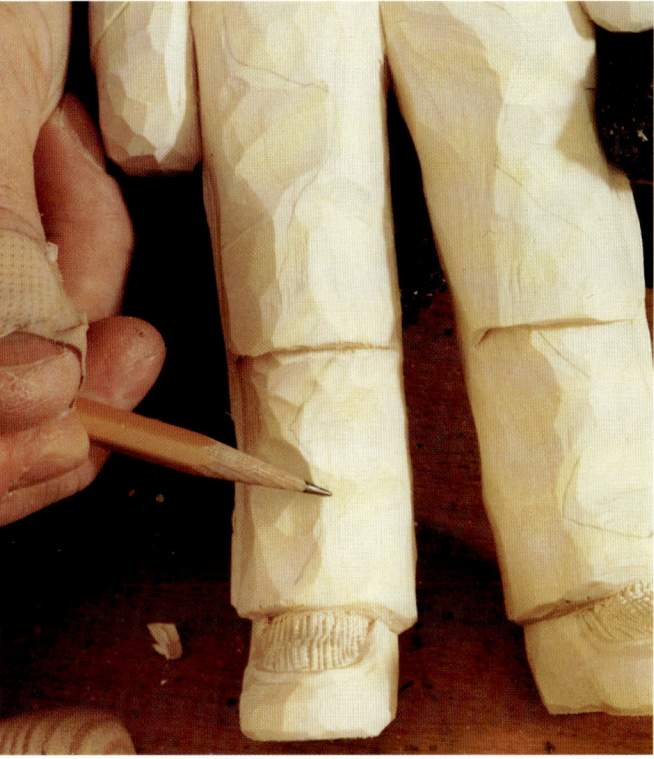

Along the legs of the pants, the wrinkles will generally form a crest that extends from the waist to the knee and from the knee to the bottom of the pant leg in the form of a zigzag. So, we'll draw this zigzag onto the leg and use knives and gouges to relieve the leg on either side of this zigzag line.

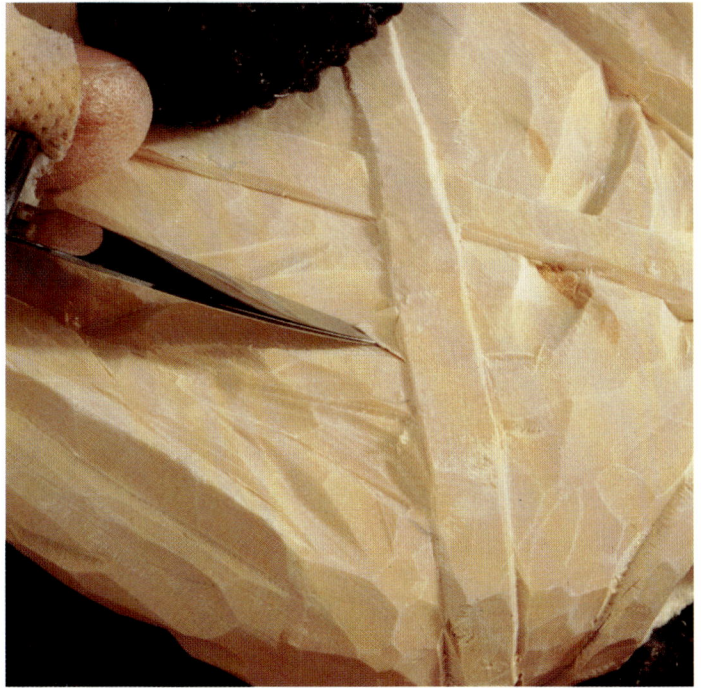

Again, use your large V tool to cut along the flow of the wrinkles and a large gouge to broaden and deepen these V cuts. When it is possible, use your knife tip to extend these wrinkles under the straps along the back and the front of the buckskin shirt.

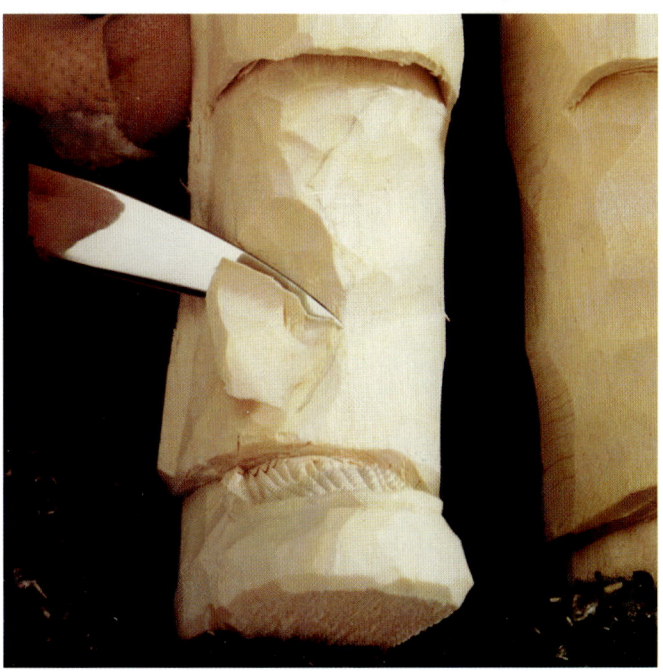

First relieve one side of the line ...

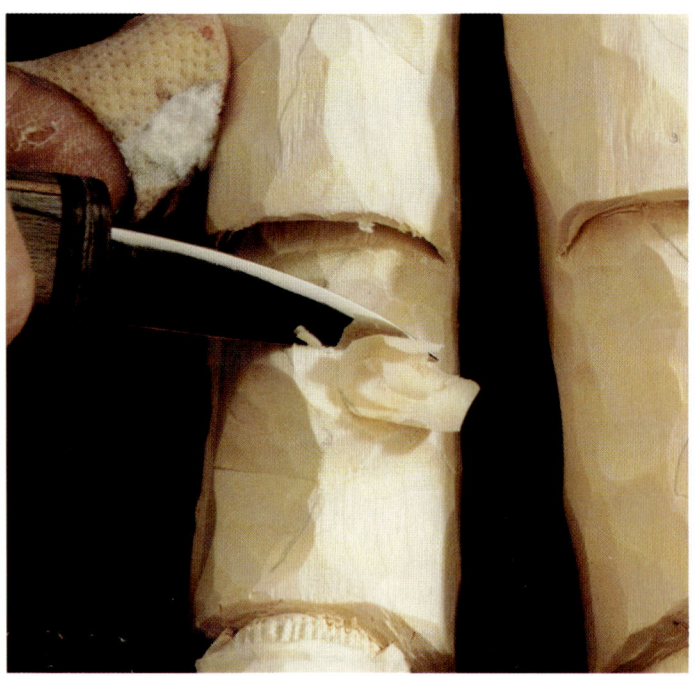

and then the opposite side of the line.

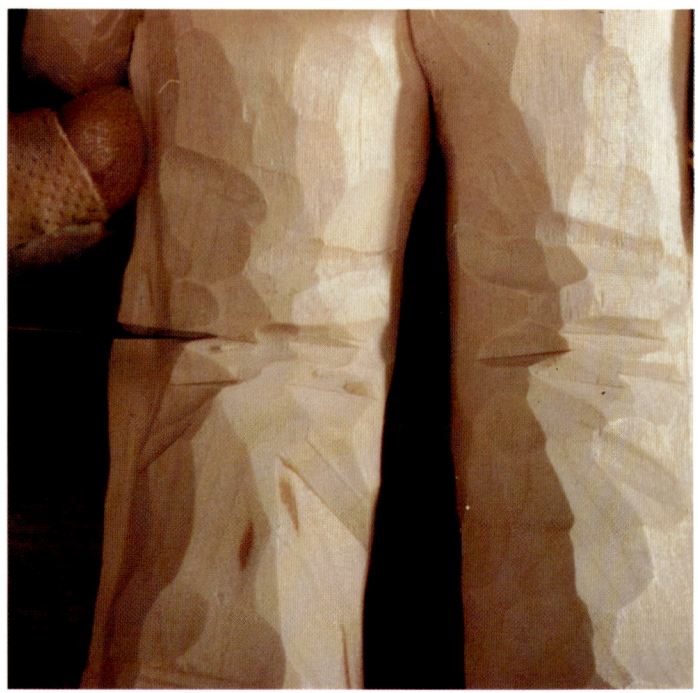

On the back of each leg, there will be a series of very tight wrinkles behind the knees and looser wrinkles radiating from that knee area over the length of the pant line.

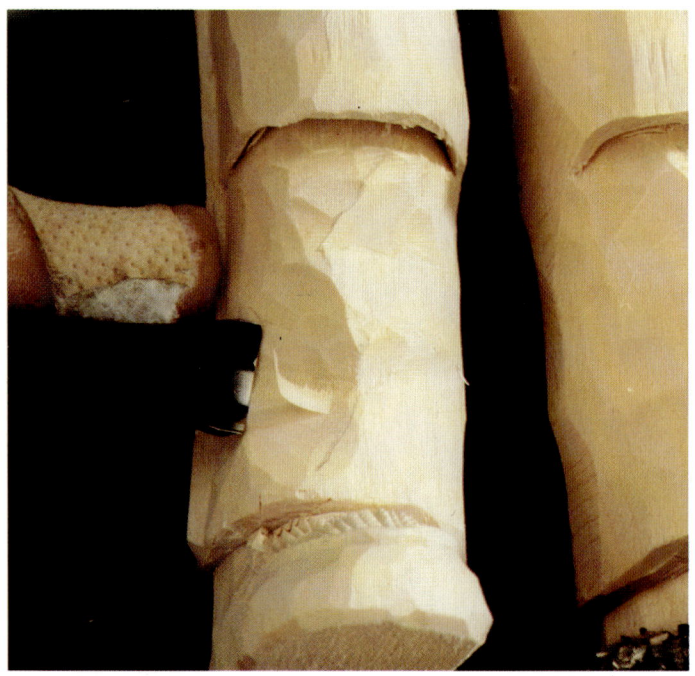

Use a large gouge to soften the valleys of these wrinkles.

The looser wrinkles along the back of the pant legs are in place, along with the rest of the wrinkles over the back of the body.

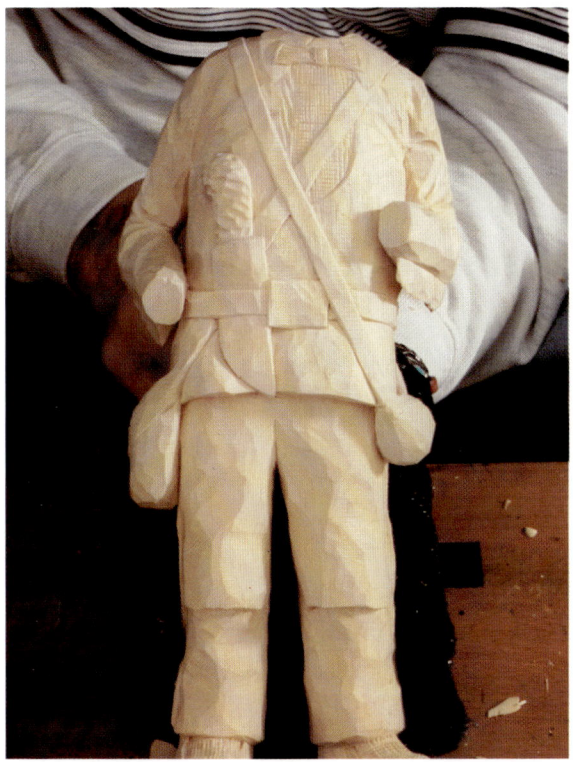

The completed wrinkles along the mountain man's front.

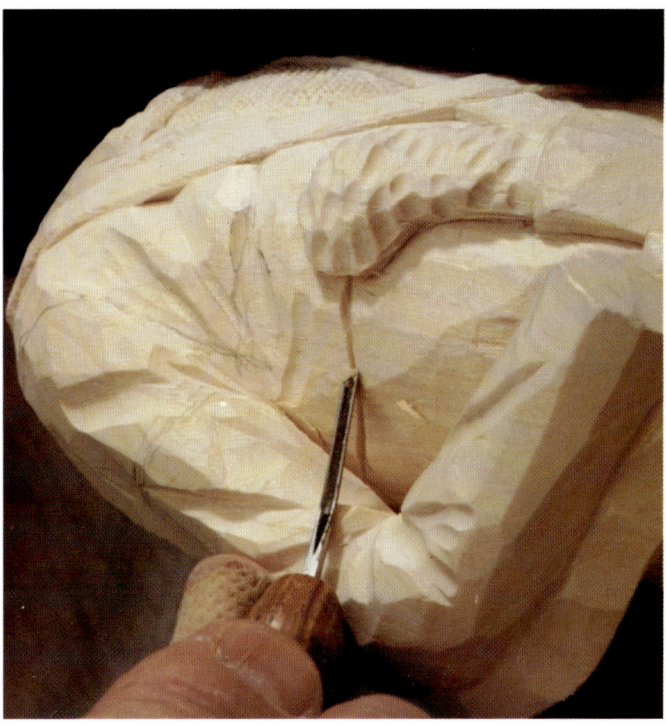

With a small V tool, score along the bottom of the fringe.

It is time to carve the fringe around the buckskin shirt. These lines represent the top and bottom of the fringe.

Then relieve the shirt up to this V cut.

Use your small V tool to cut fringe in along the front of the shirt as shown here...

over the shoulders,...

along the back of the shirt,...

and along the backs of the arms.

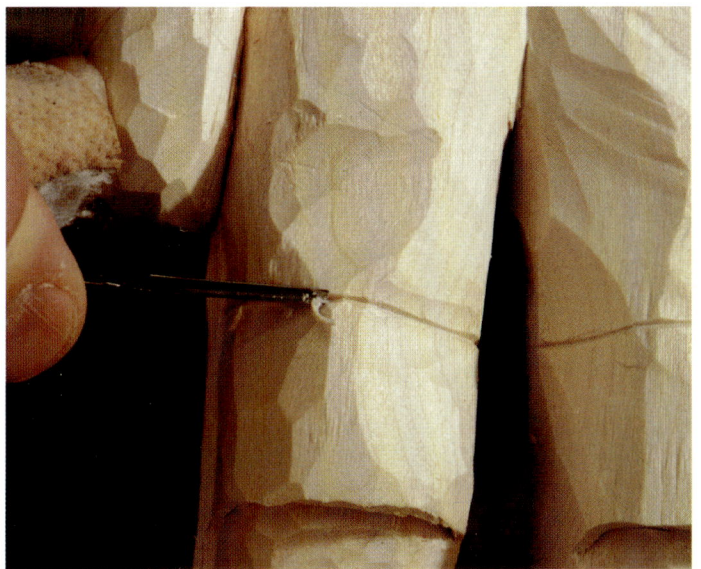

Use a V tool to score along the upper limit of the knee fringe.

Again, use your V tool to cut in the fringe.

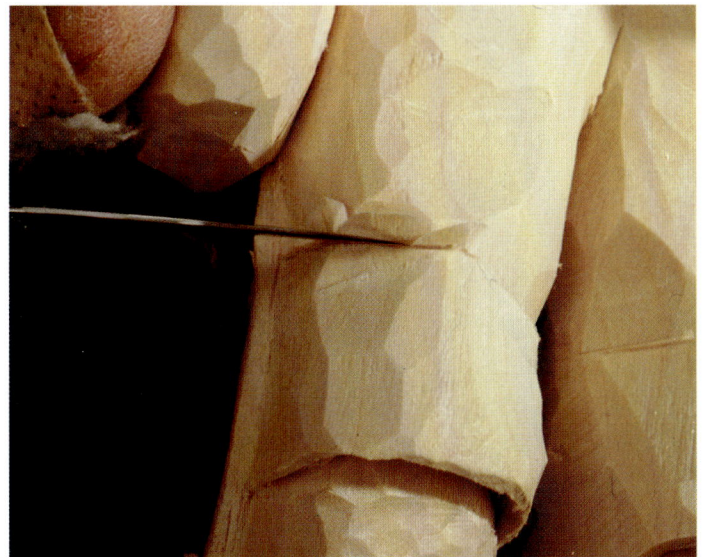

Relieve the leg down to this V cut.

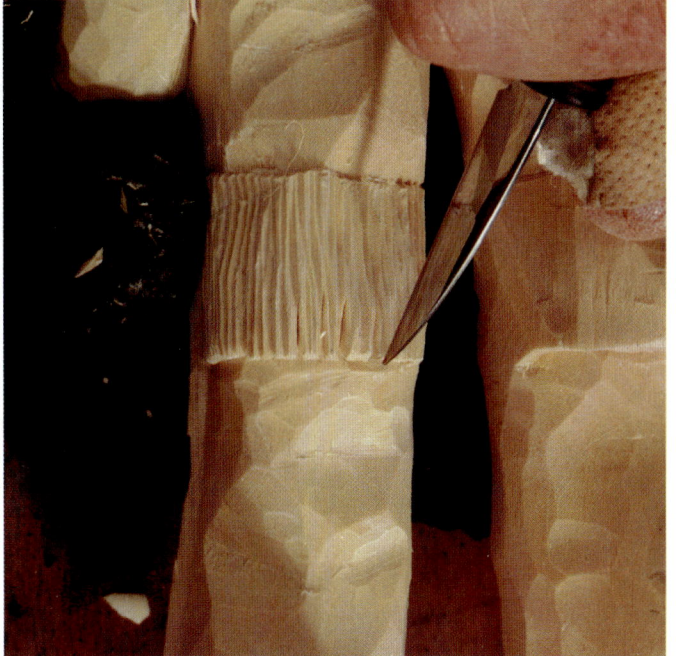

We undercut the knee earlier. By separating some of the fringe along this undercut we will create some shadows and consequently some extra interest along this fringe.

Don't forget the fringe along the outside of the pant legs.

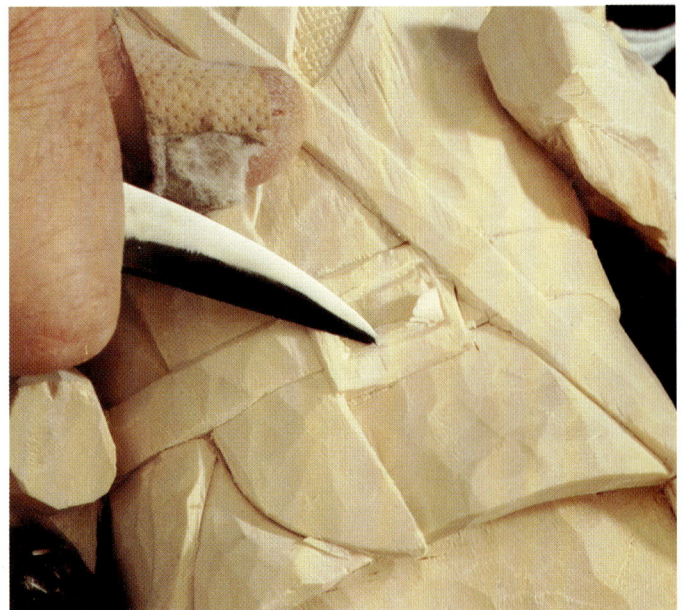

Use a knife to relieve the buckle itself, removing excess wood from the center portion of the buckle.

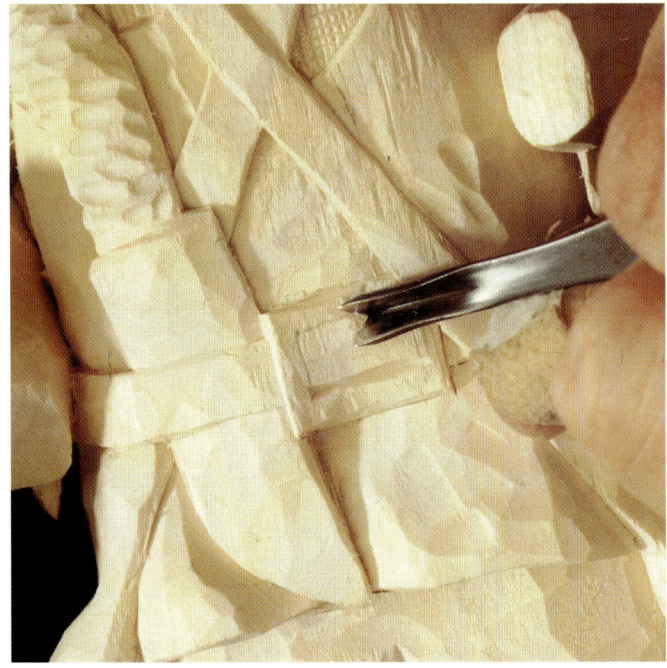

The last detail to complete on the body is the belt buckle. First use a V tool to outline the area to be relieved.

The carving of the body is complete.

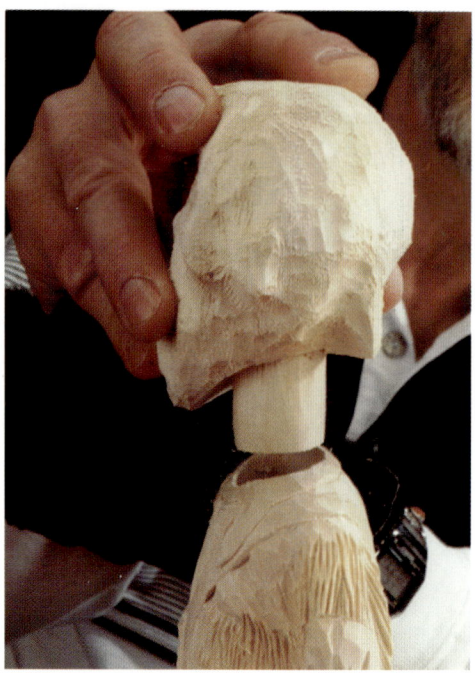

The first order of business on the head is to carve the neck to the 1" diameter that will allow it to fit snugly into the neck hole. Note the angle of the beard, which has been cut in toward the neck. This beard shape reflects the same angle that the chest makes to the neck hole.

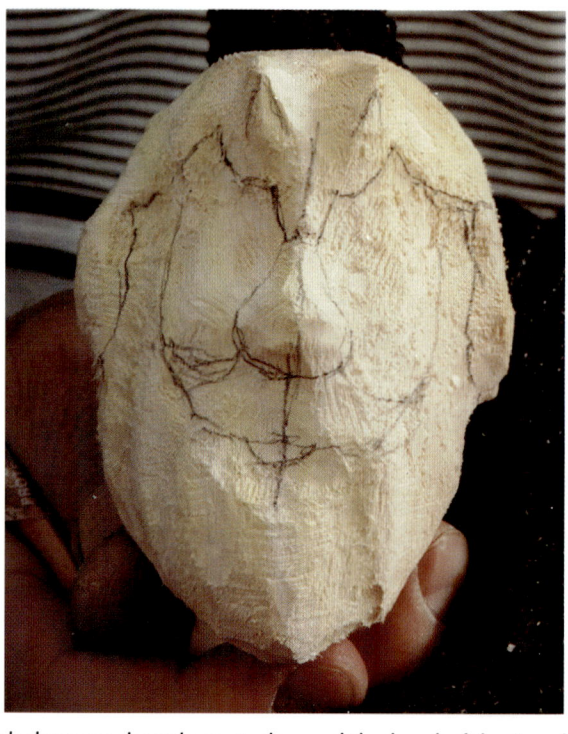

Sketch the nose, beard, mustache, and the head of the "road kill" cap on to the front view of the head.

The head is inserted into the body. Note how the beard follows the angle of the body.

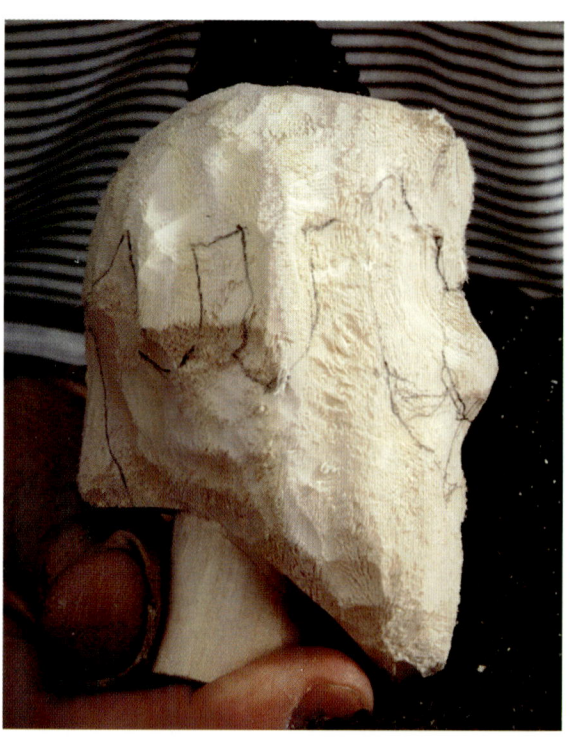

In a similar manner, we'll sketch the details of the road kill legs and tail onto the side view.

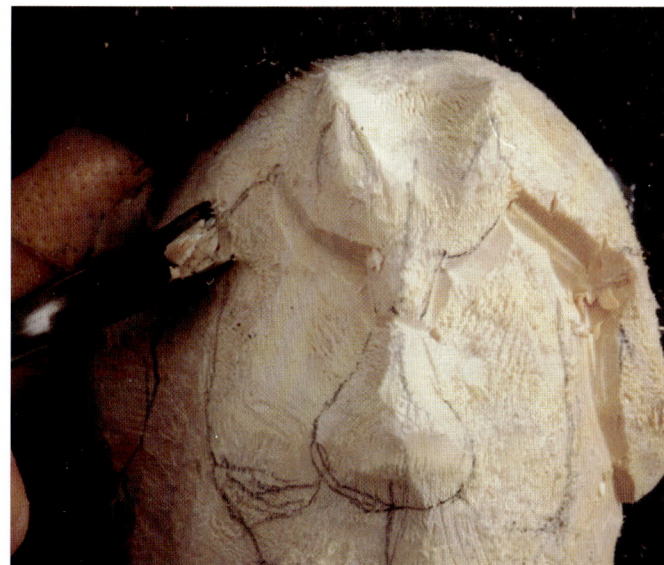

We're going to complete the cap before we carve the face, so let's outline the body, legs and head of the animal with a large V tool.

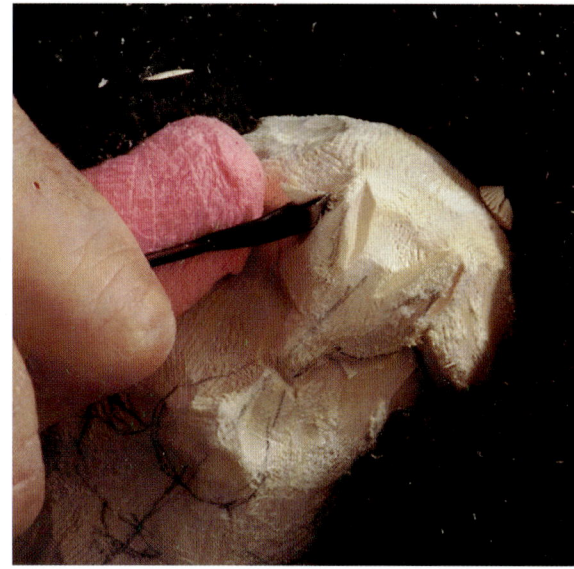

On the road kill head, cut the pointed ears in using a V tool...

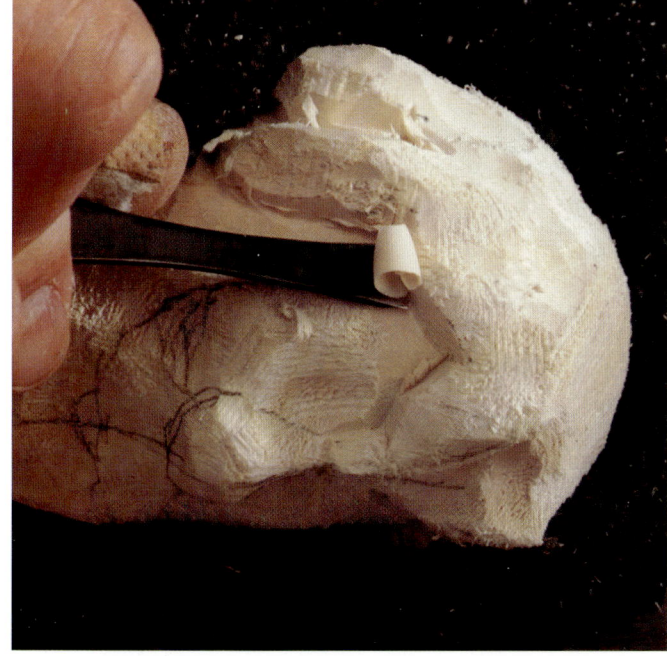

To relieve the head to the outline of the cap, use a 1/2" or smaller fishtail gouge. You will notice in this shot that I don't have that flaming pink protection on my thumb. After having heard Mr. Snyder complaining about the appearance of my Band-Aid, I have decided to use the gaudy, pink "wimp wrap" from this point on.

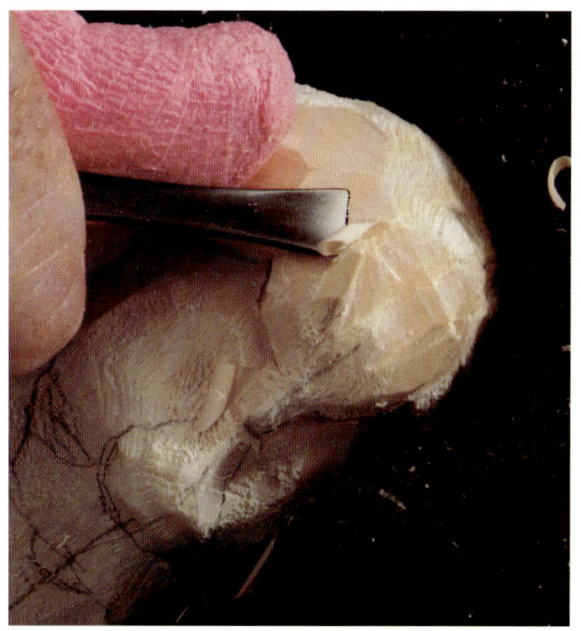

and then relieve the head around these ears using the 1/2" fishtail.

Extend the legs up on the sides of the animal's body.

and its legs.

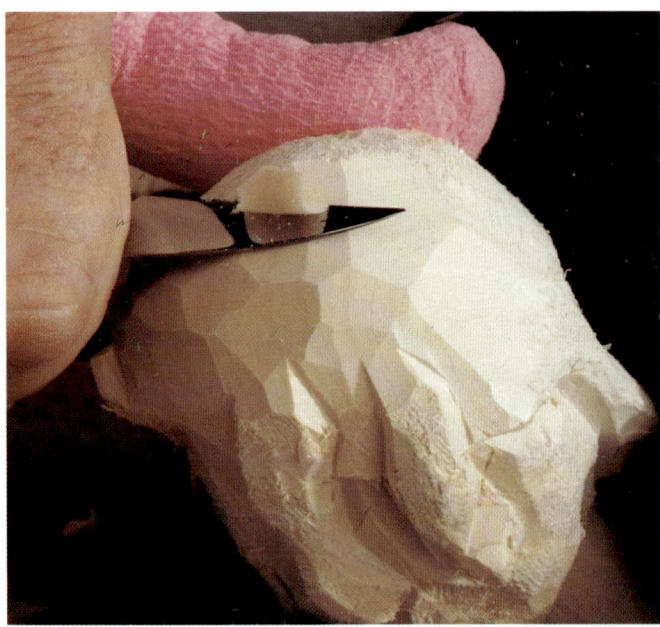

Use your knife and/or gouges to clean burr and saw marks from the animal's body...

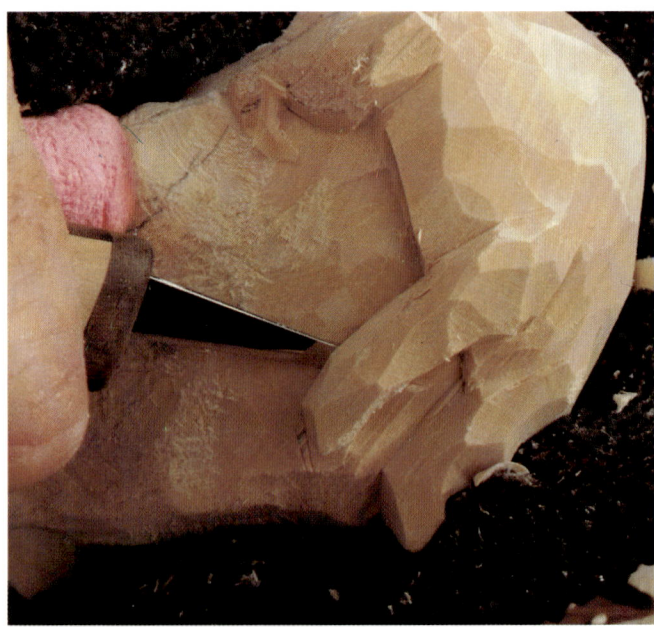

Begin to separate each of the legs from the side of the head. This is a slow process and should be done very carefully or else the legs will break. The following is a sample vocabulary for you to use if you do break the leg: "##%**!!!"

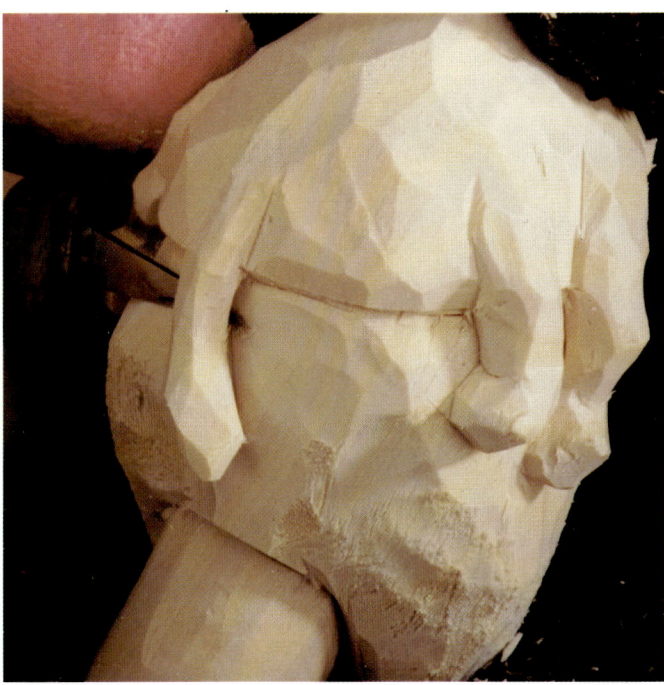

Let's separate the tail from the back of the mountain man's head.

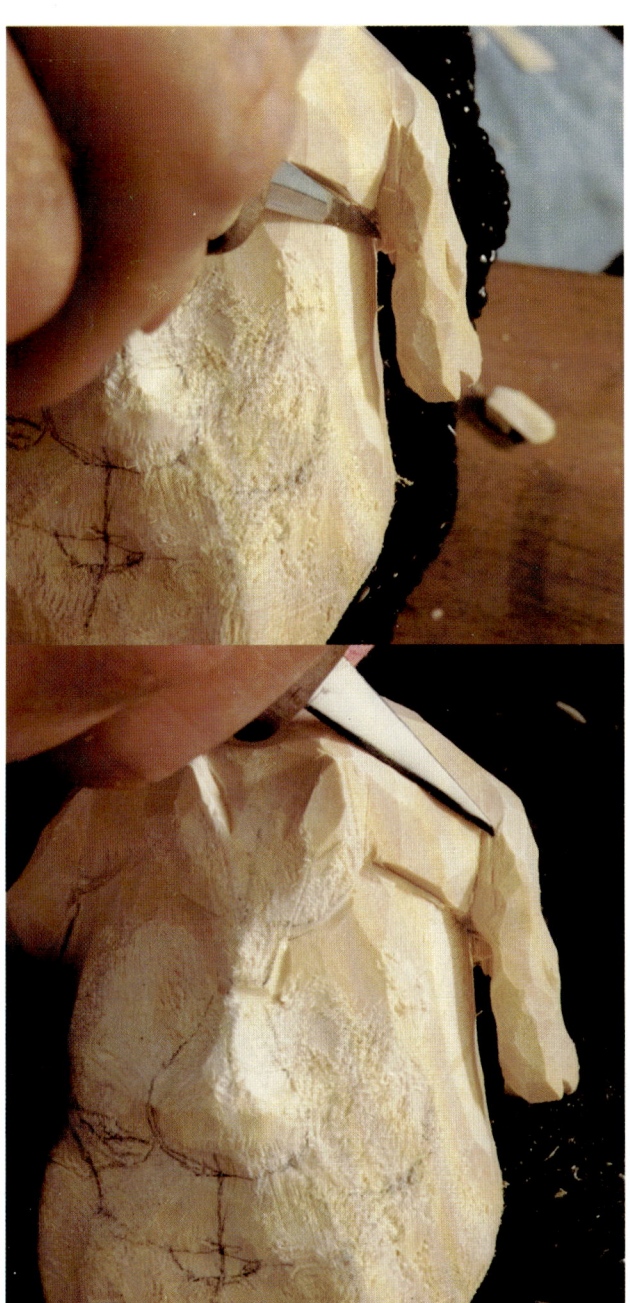

The legs are separated from the head.

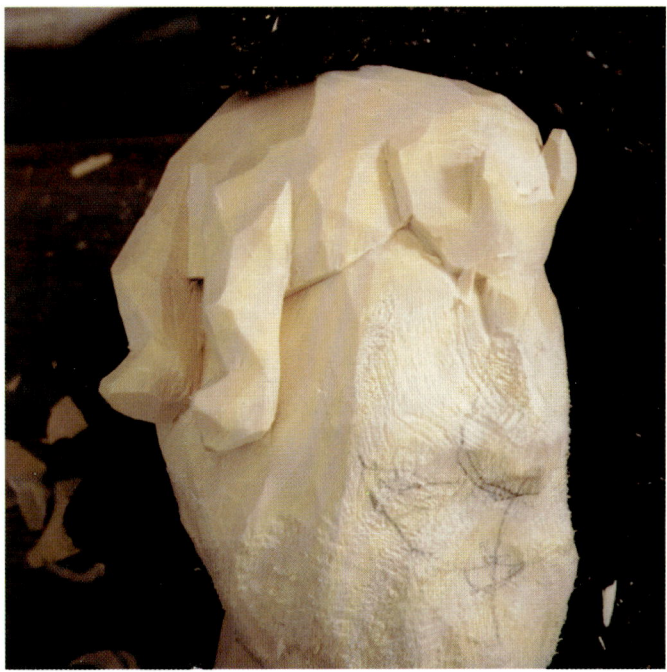

On the right side of the head, severely undercut the legs but do not separate them entirely from the side of the head.

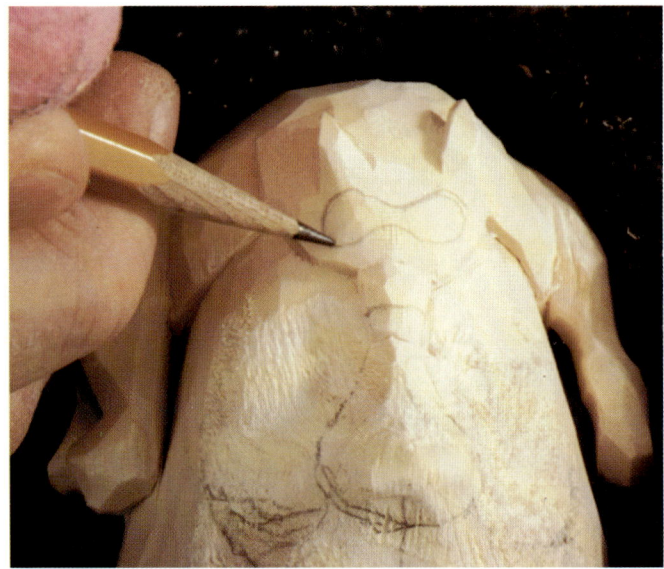

We'll sketch the eyes on so that there is no separation between the cornea.

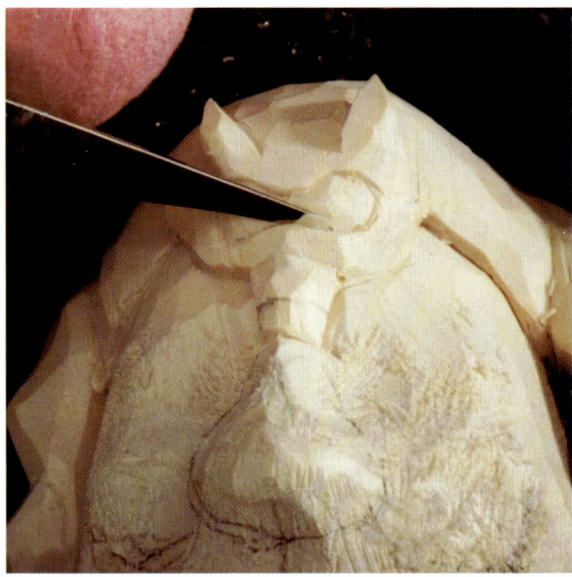

Use your detail knife to relieve the cornea.

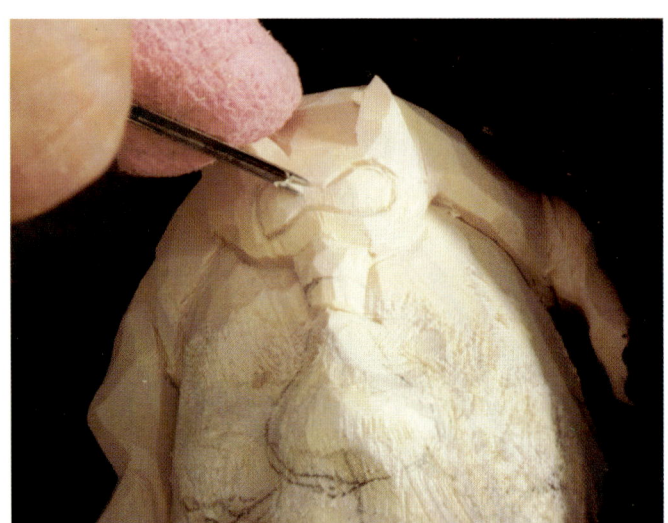

Use a small V to outline the eyes.

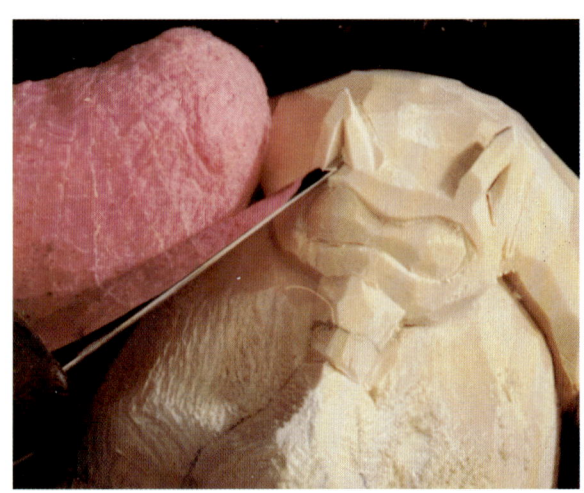

Use your knife to chip out a small triangle in the front of each ear.

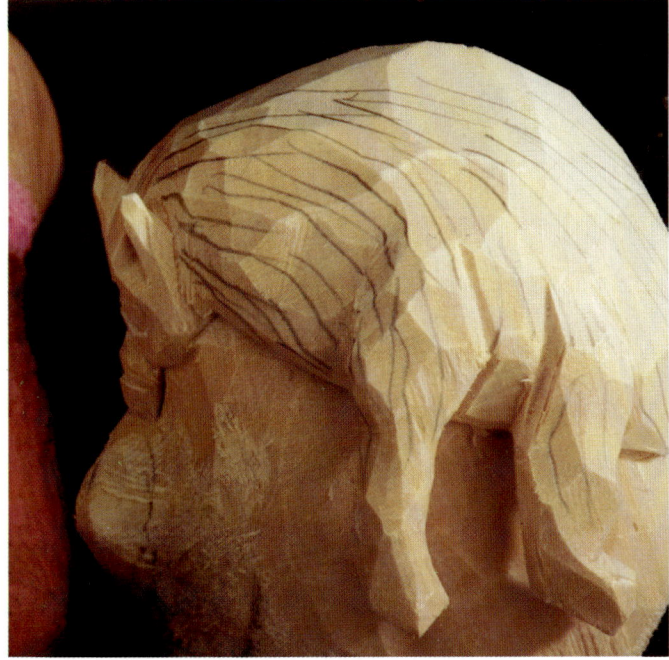

The hair track on this animal will generally follow the lines I've drawn.

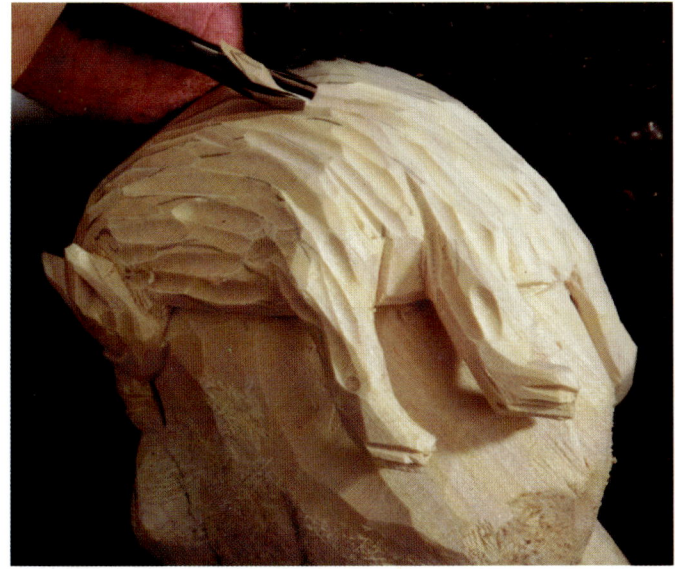

Use a 1/8" deep gouge to carve the fur. Note the small toenails on the feet. These were formed using a small V tool.

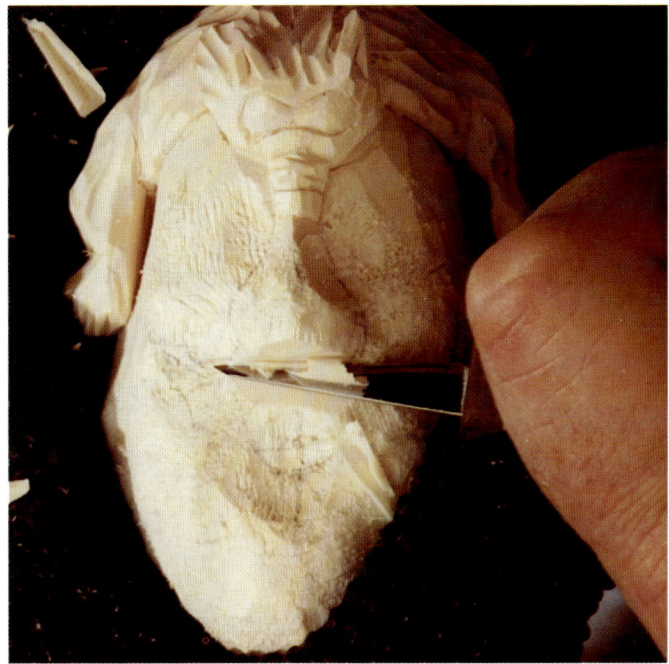

To begin carving the face, first clip off the bottom of the nose.

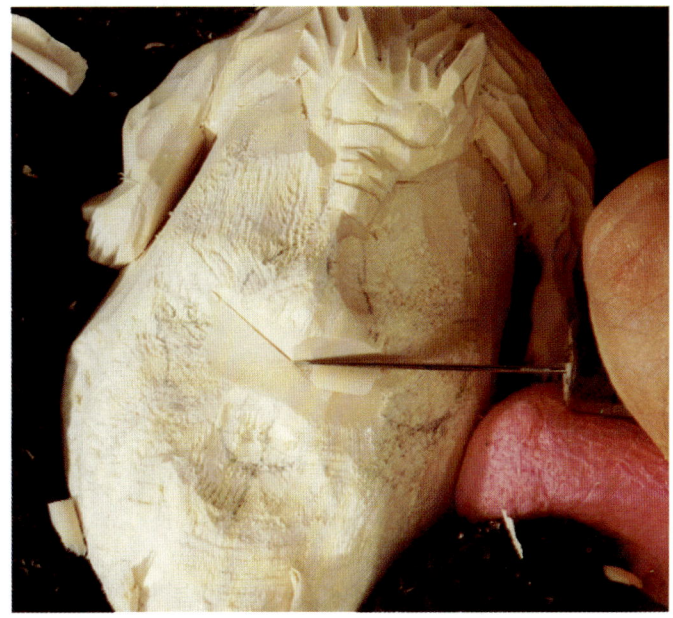

Note the angle at which the bottom of the nose is cut

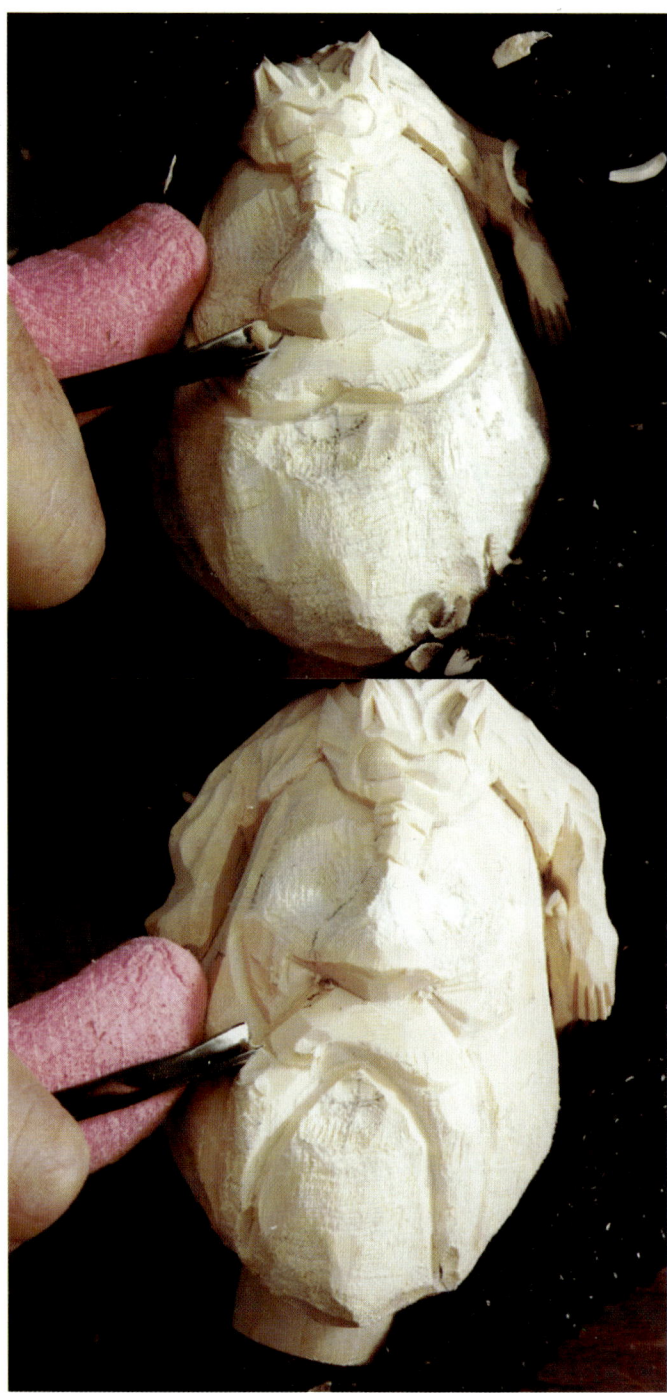

Draw in the outline of the beard and mustache. Cut along these lines with a large V tool. If you don't like the looks of the mustache the way you have drawn it in, it certainly isn't difficult to change when you start carving.

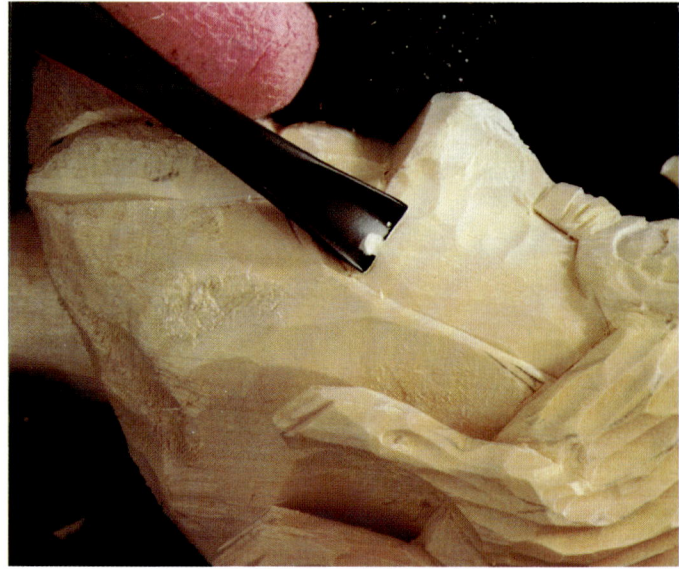

Relieve the face to the V cut that outlines the hair.

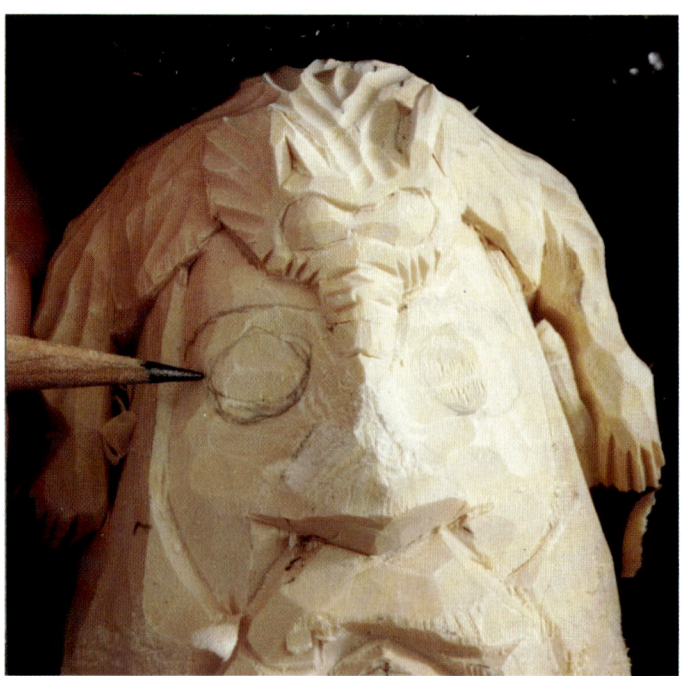

Sketch in the general location for each eye.

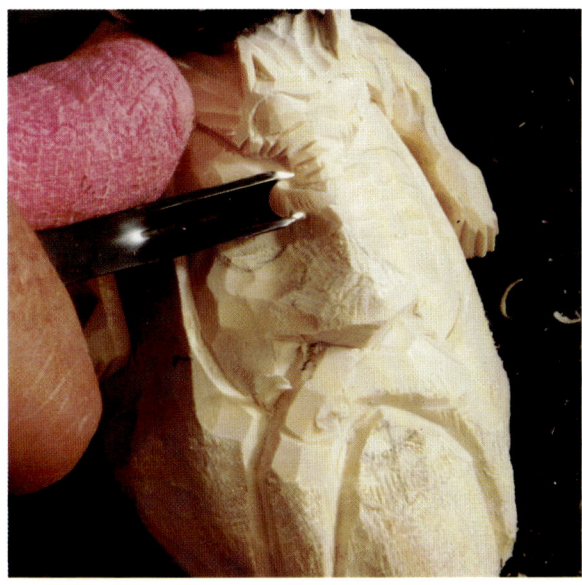

Use a 1/4" deep gouge to cut in the eye sockets. This eye socket should be cut in straight across the head, perpendicular to the flat plane that would separate the head into two equal pieces.

The smile line is in place.

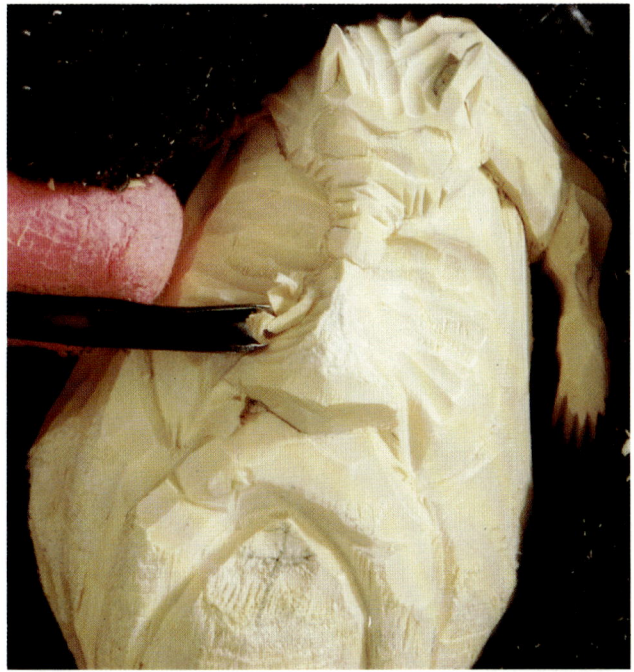

Use this same gouge to clean burr marks off the nose. Also use your V tool to cut smile lines into the sides of the nose.

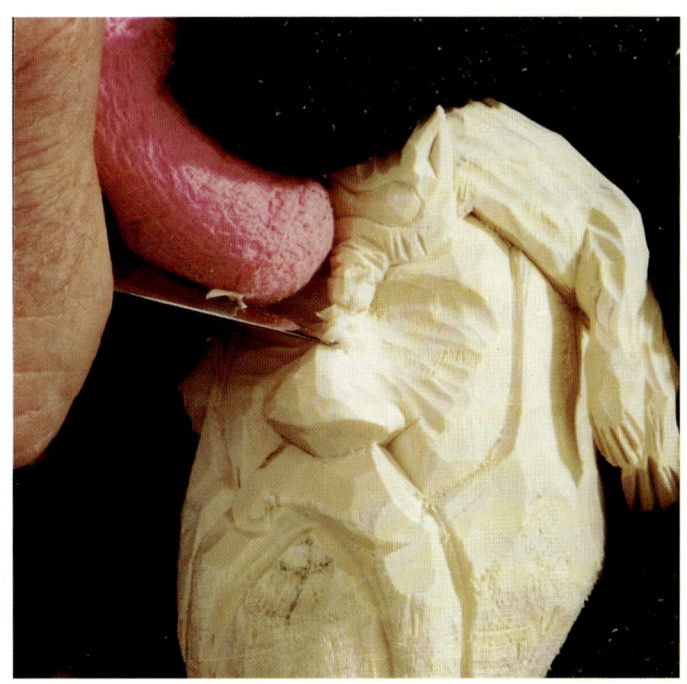

Use your knife to shape the nose.

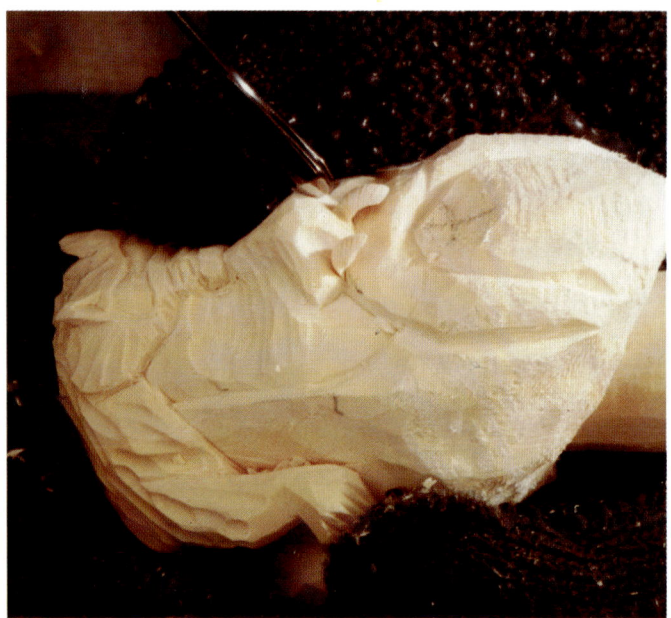

Use your 1/4" gouge to cut in nostrils.

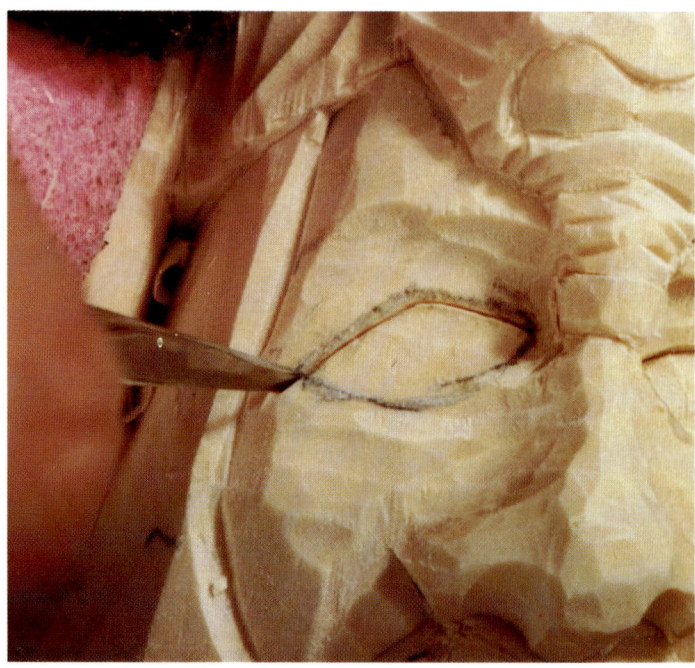

First outline the eye with your knife tip.

Sketch in the eyes.

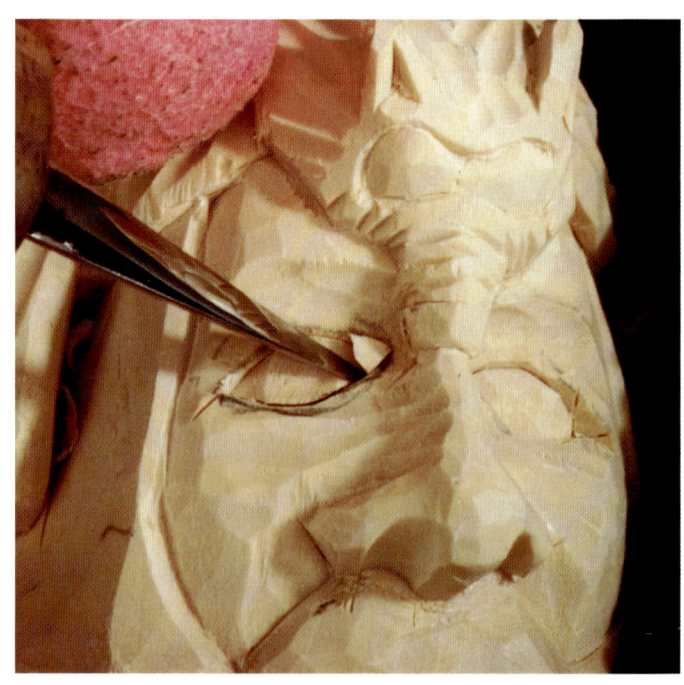

Carefully remove the inside and outside corners of the eyeball. Note the angle of the blade.

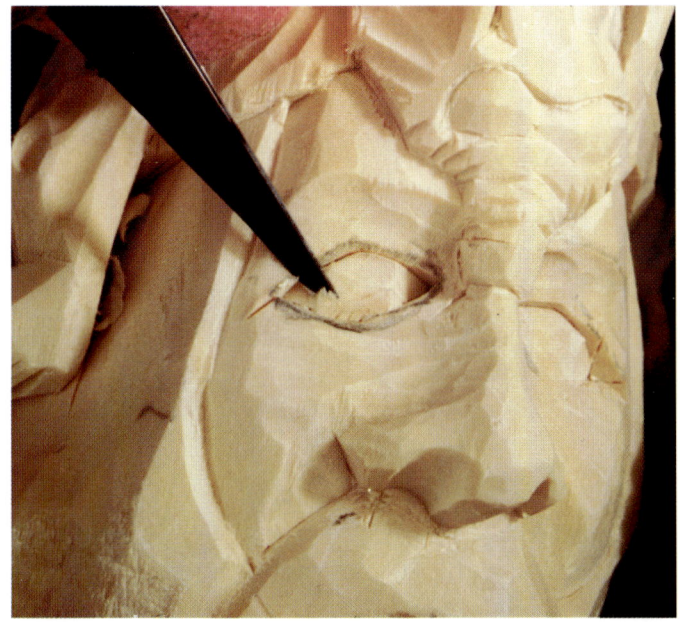

Relieve the eyeball from about the middle of the eye to the lower eyelid.

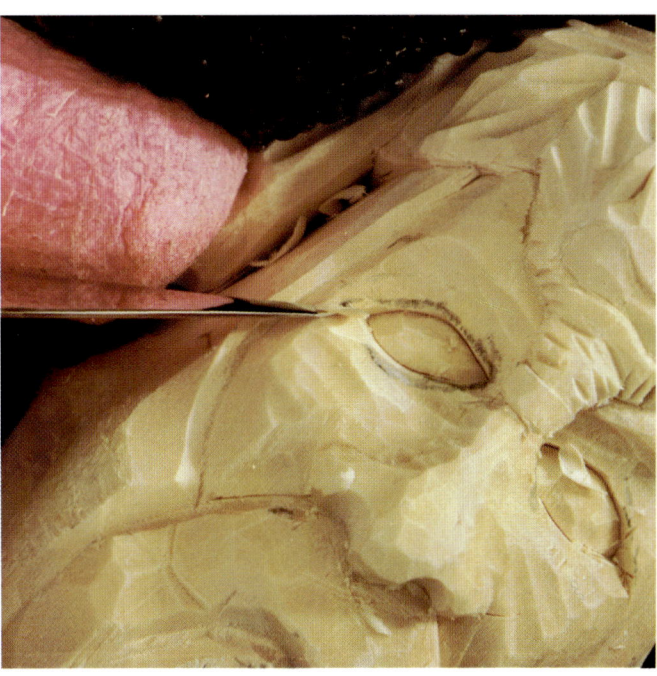

Clip out the outside corner underneath the upper lid. This results in the upper lid overhanging the lower lid.

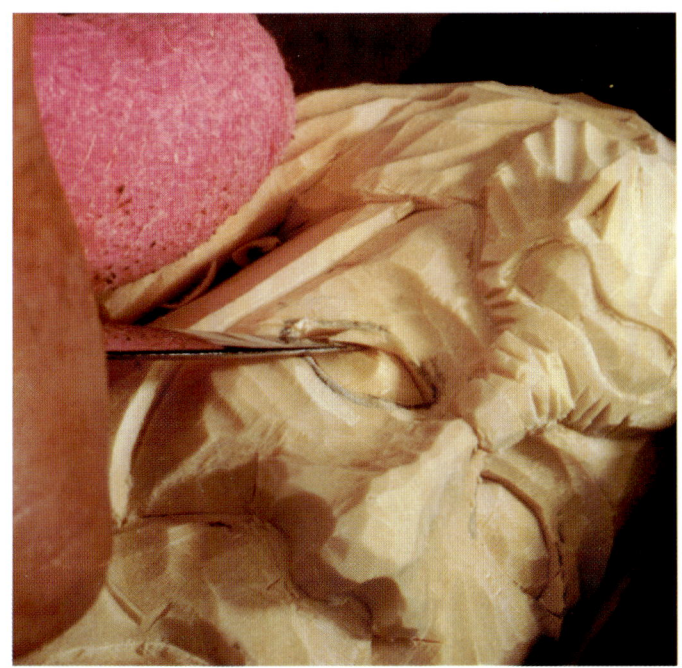

Then relieve the eyeball from the approximate middle of the eye to the upper eyelid.

With a medium size V tool, follow the curvature of the eyeball and create the upper lid

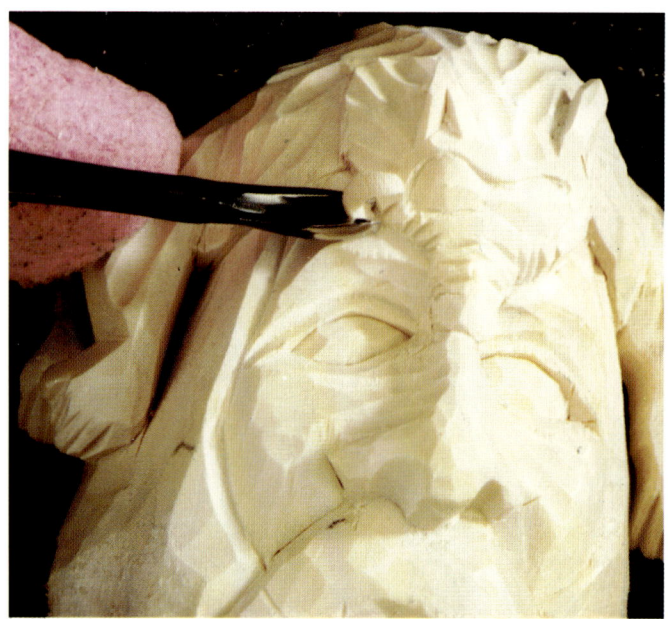

With your small, deep gouge, form a mound above each eye. You will carve hair for the eyebrows into each mound.

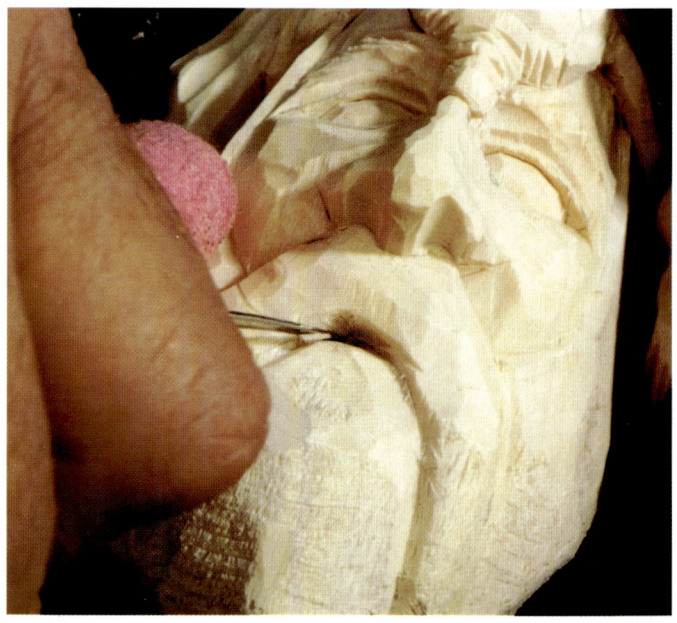

Chip out a small triangle of wood directly underneath the nose and adjacent to the underside of the mustache.

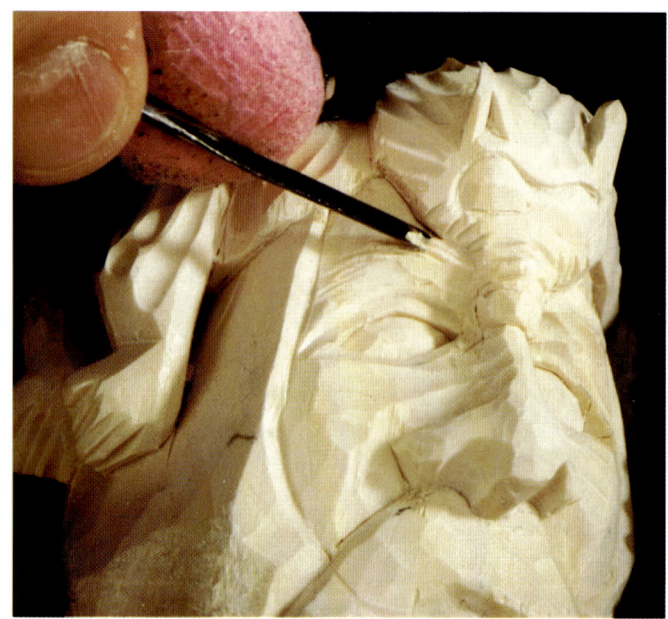

Use a small V tool to form the hair on the eyebrow mounds.

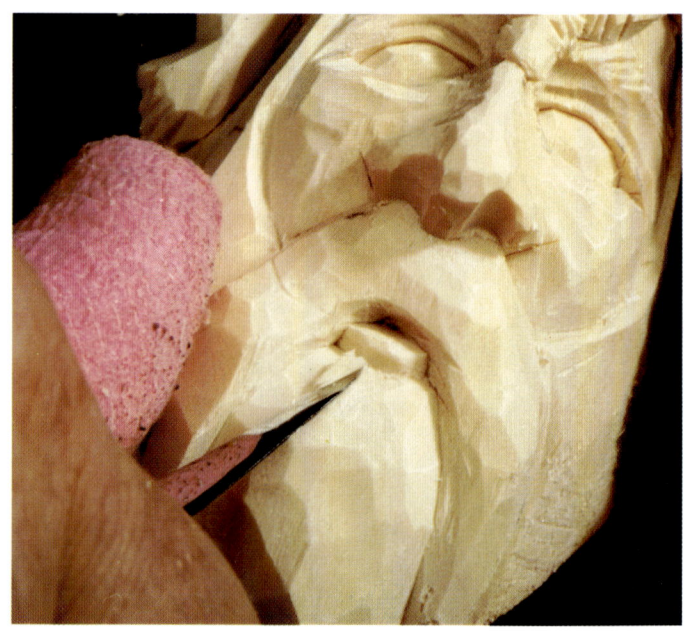

Use your knife to form a lower lip around this triangular opening.

Use your knife to relieve the beard from around the mustache and to clean off all remaining burr and saw marks from the beard and mustache.

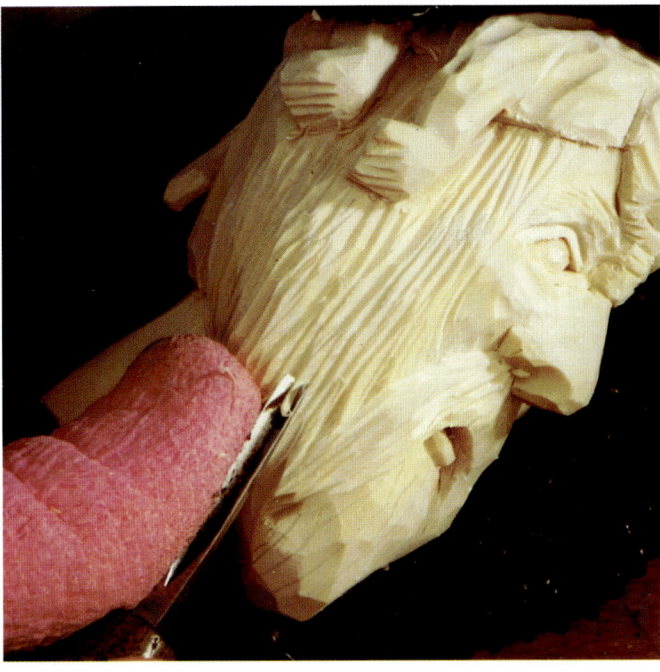

Use a small to medium size V tool or a small deep gouge to cut the hair in. In general follow the flow of the hair, but don't make all of your cuts parallel to each other. Nor do you want all of the cuts to be of the same depth or length.

Sketch in the flow of the hair for the beard and mustache.

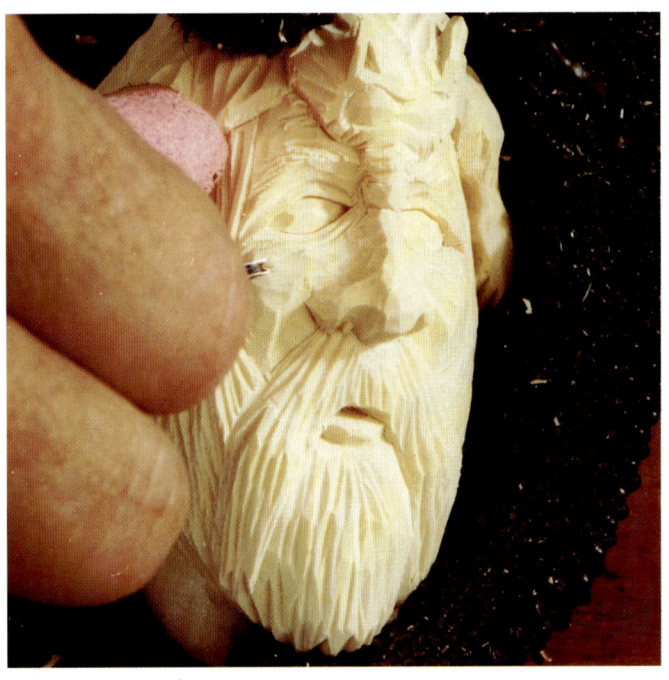

Use your small V tool to add some wrinkles around the eyes.

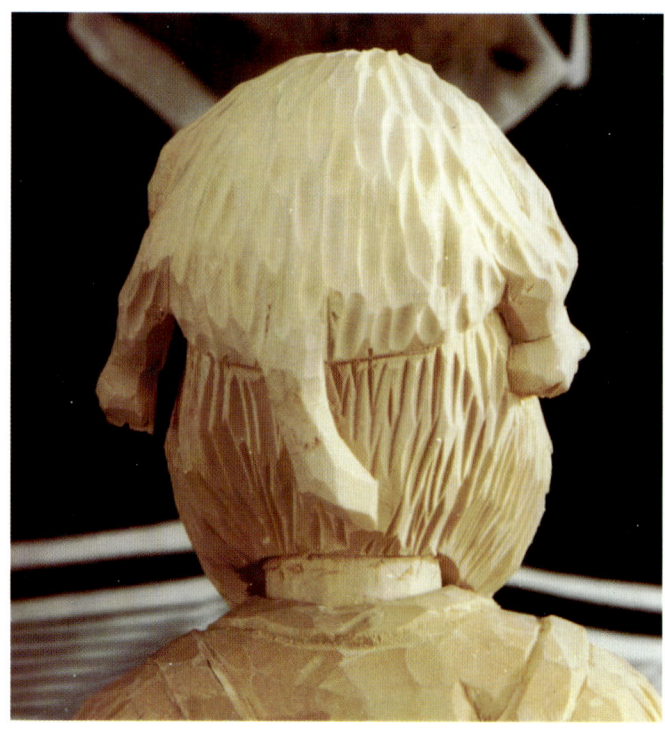

The completed head.

42

Let's carve the gloved hands to fit the body now.

Round off the back of the glove.

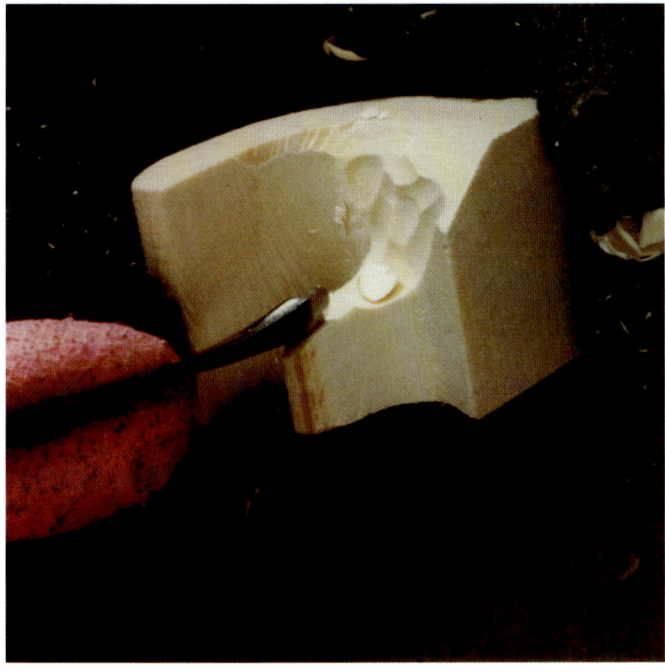

Use a large, deep gouge to cut the thumb in.

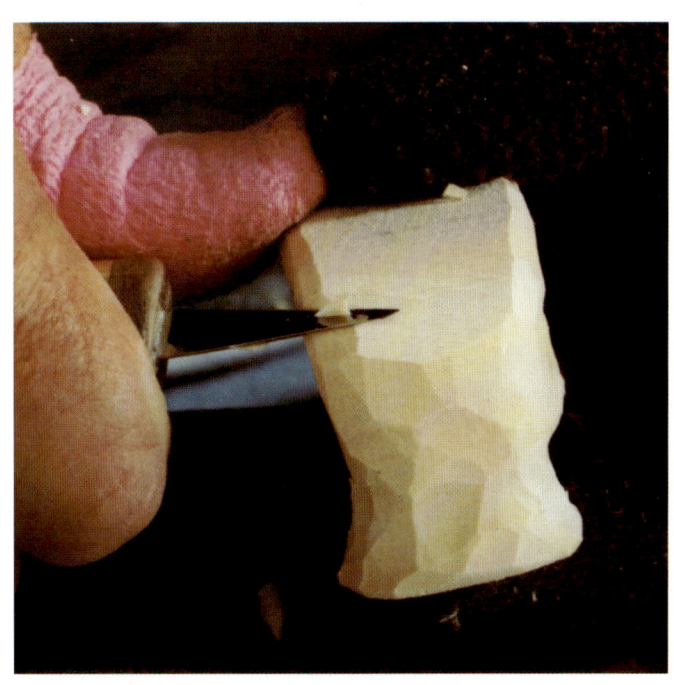

Here we have flared the hand opening to the glove and are cleaning saw marks from the finger section of the glove.

Lay out the four fingers on the hand. Remember that the length of each finger varies.

Use your medium sized V tool to separate the fingers and use your knife to cut the fingers to length.

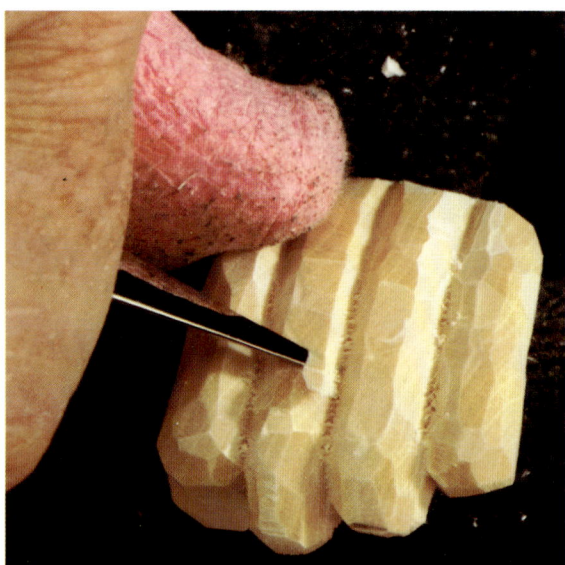

Use your knife to round off the fingers along the edges of the V cuts.

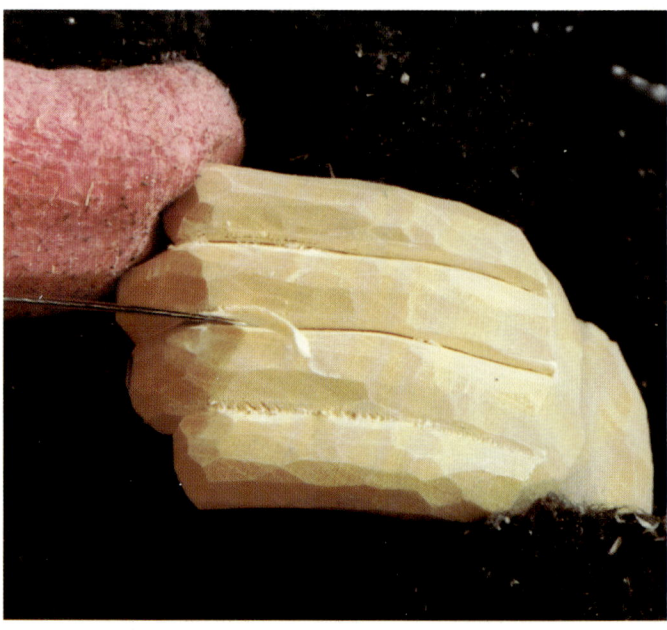

Use the knife tip to enhance the valleys separating the fingers.

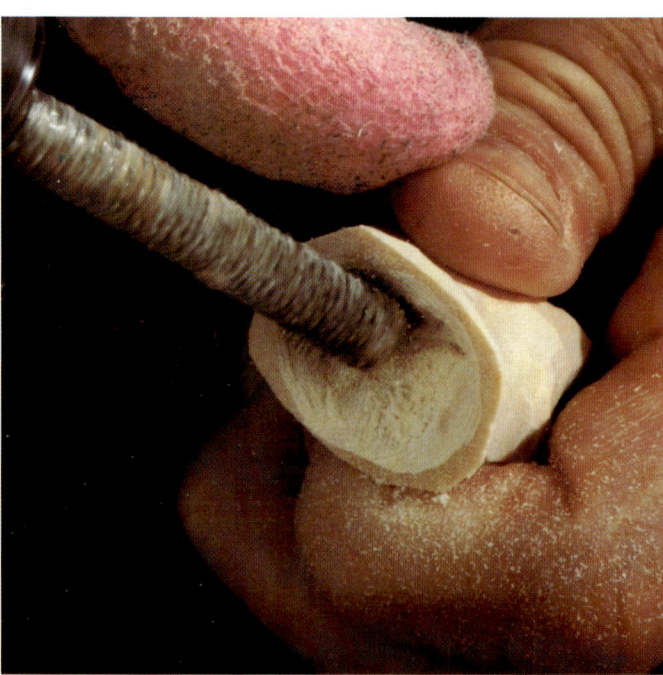

Depress the inside of the glove to receive the arm using a 1/4" Kutzall Burr on a Foredom Flexible Shaft machine.

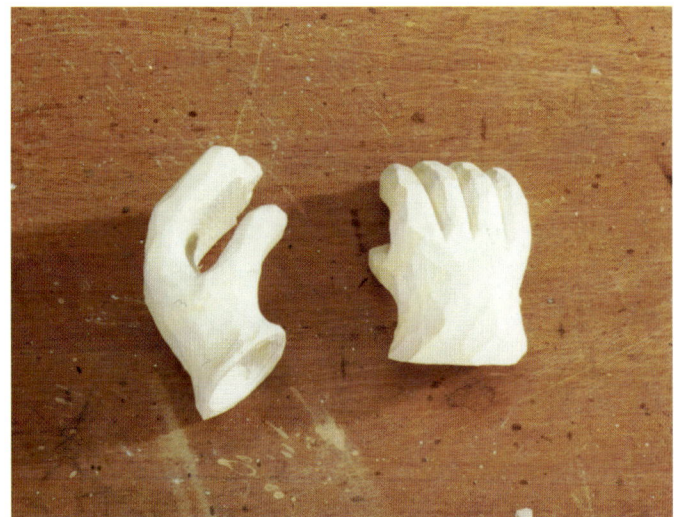

Carve the other gloved hand to match.

Drill a 1/8" hole into both the rear of the glove and into each arm.

Insert a dowel into each arm and fit the glove over the exposed remainder of the dowel.

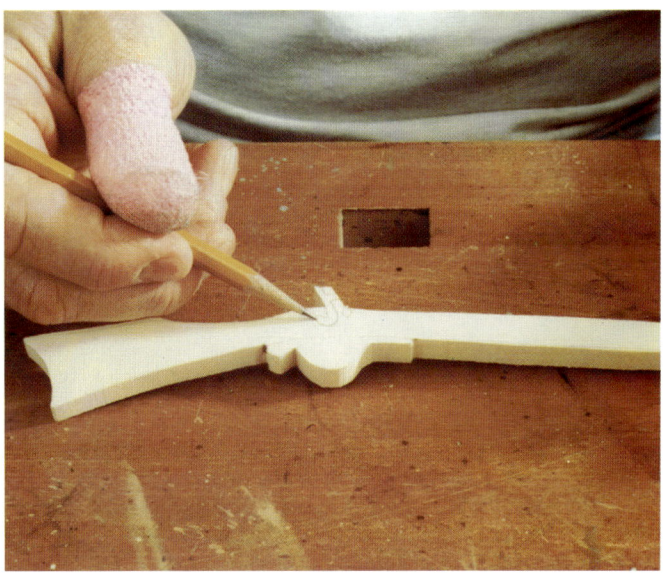

To begin carving the rifle, we need to identify the hammer.

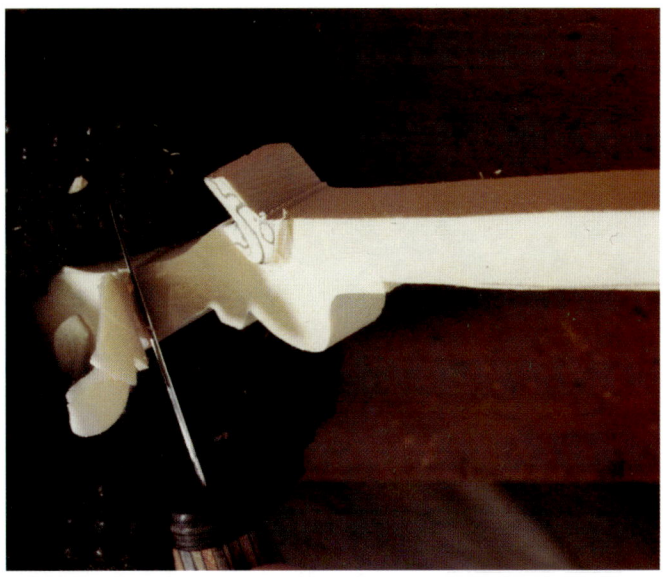

Score around the area of the hammer with your medium sized V tool and relieve the rest of the gun down to the depth of that V cut.

45

Draw a center line along the gun and remove a portion of the hammer as shown in this photo.

Draw in the details of the gun, including the trigger and the trigger guard.

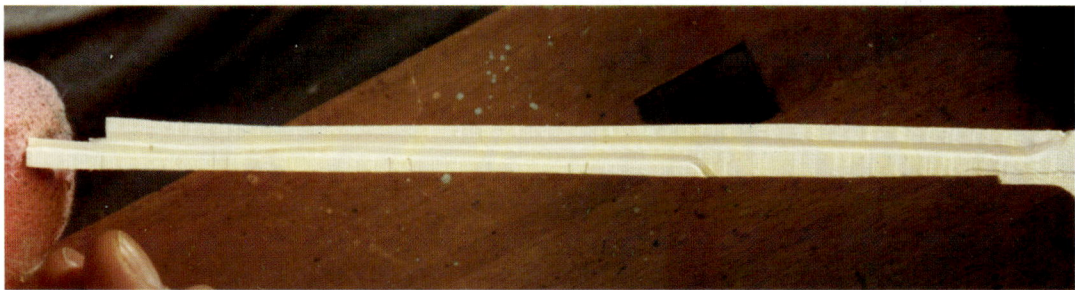
Use your V tool to outline the rifle barrel and the ramrod.

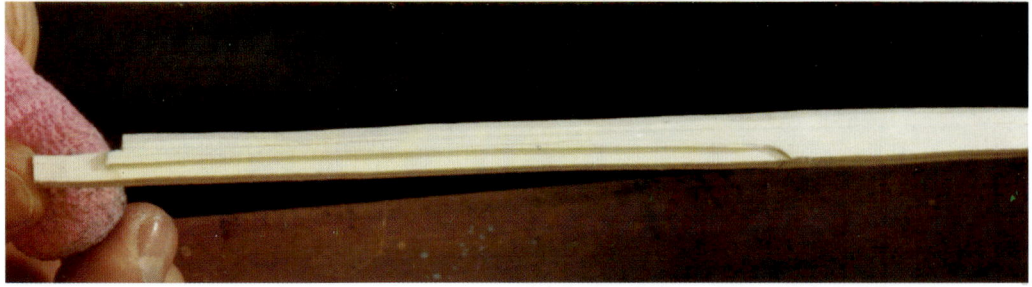
Use your knife to relieve both the barrel and the ramrod.

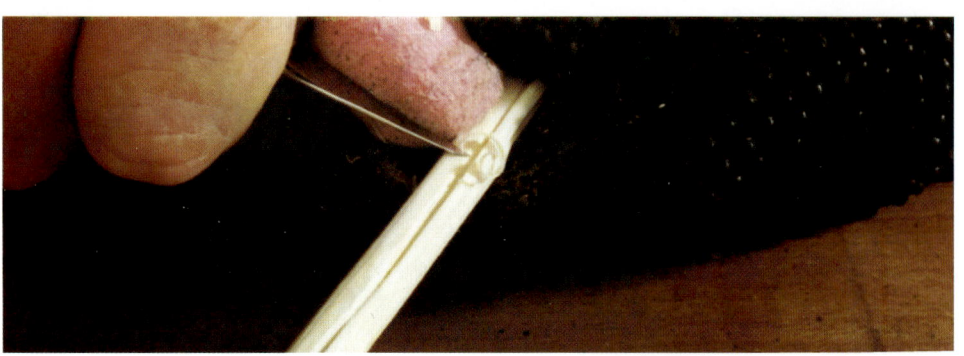
Use your knife to round both the barrel (you could make this octagon shaped if you prefer) and the ramrod.

Using a small V tool, cut in the brass holding rings for the ramrod.

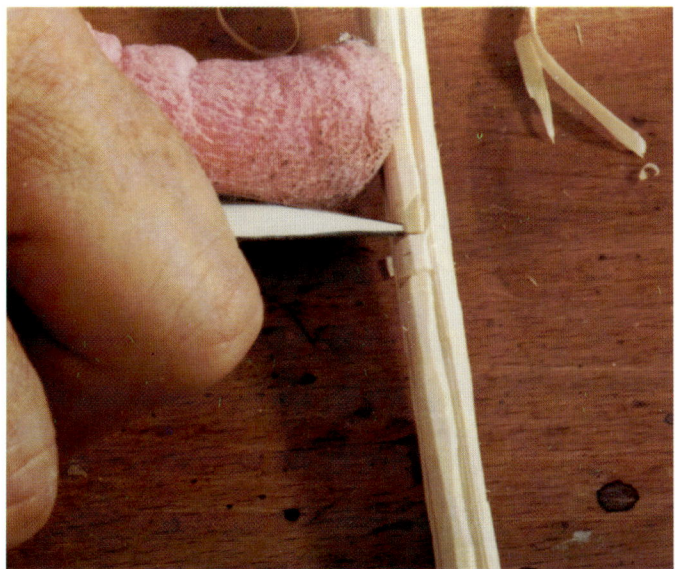

Relieve the ramrod below the thickness of the brass holding rings with your knife.

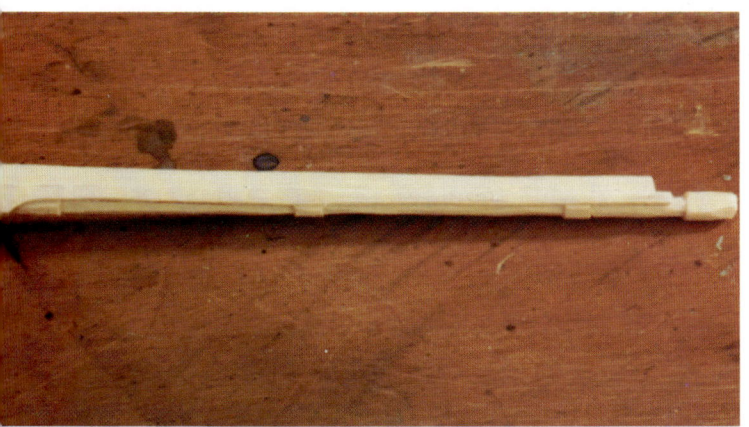

The ramrod is complete.

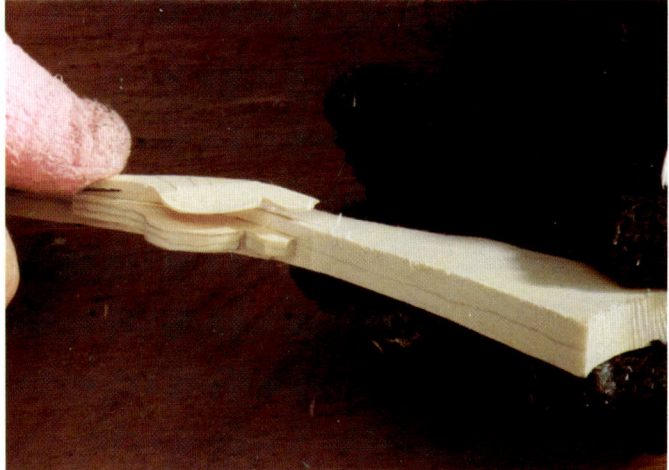

Carefully trim the trigger guard to about 1/16" thick.

Narrow the gun stock at this point to about 1/8" wide.

Round the gun stock.

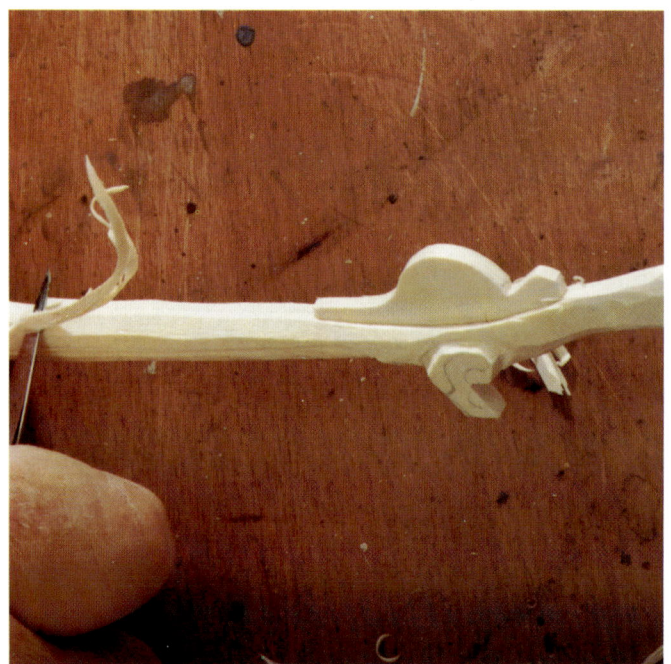

Round off the gun stock and the barrel.

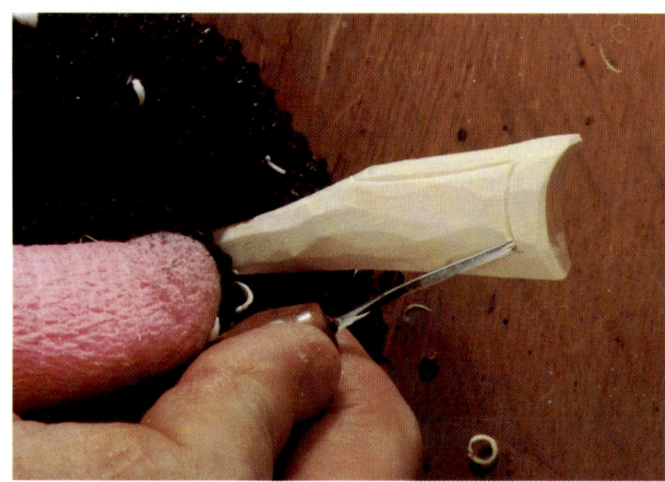

Outline the brass butt plate with your V tool.

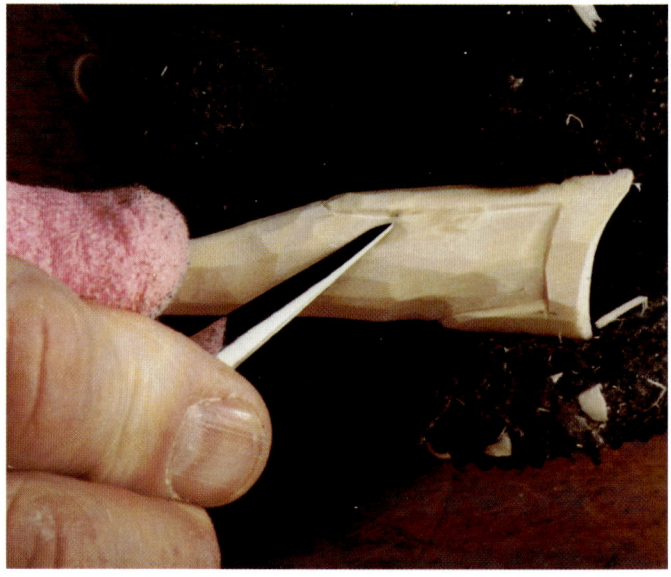

Relieve the gun stock to the butt plate with a knife.

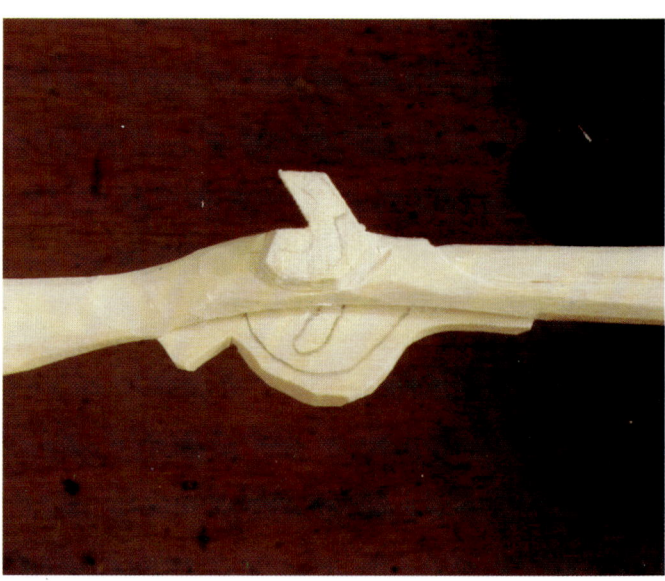

Redraw both the trigger and trigger guard.

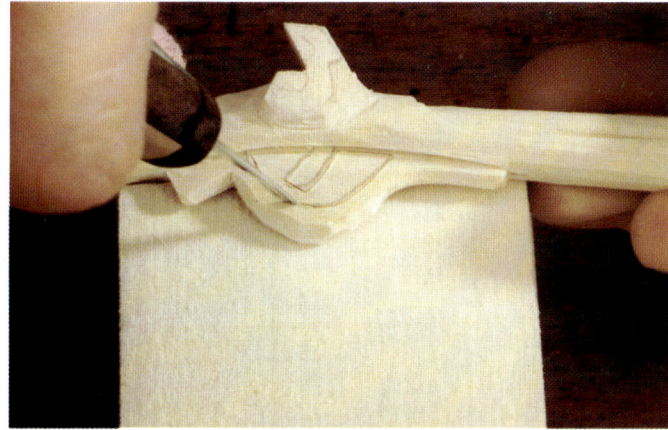

Placing the underside of the trigger guard on a block of scrap wood, use your knife tip to gently score around the trigger guard and trigger. Continue to score in same groove until the trigger guard and trigger are free.

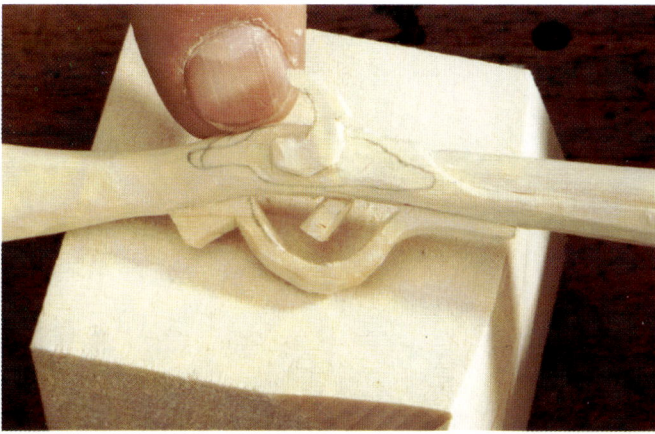

The hammer has been carved with a knife and the guard plate is sketched on. Relieve the wood away around the guard plate.

The completed firing mechanism and brass guard plate. I recommend saturating the hammer with Super Glue to prevent breakage.

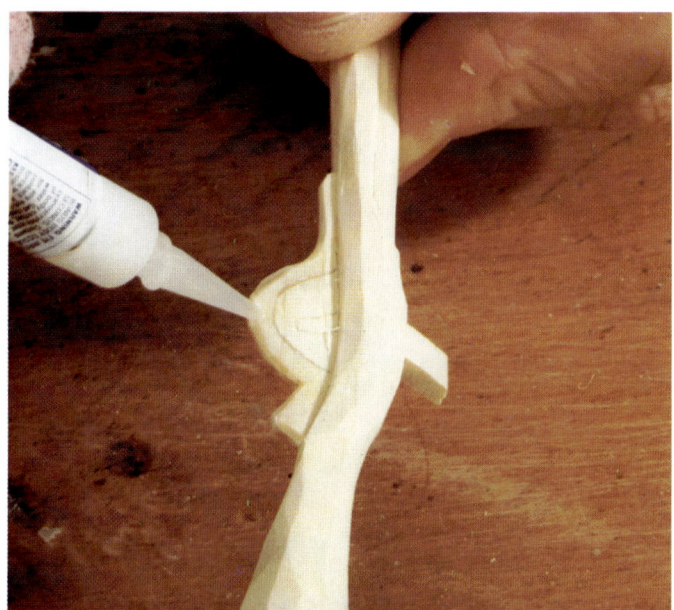

You can use Super Glue to saturate the trigger guard, reinforcing it. Allow the saturated guard to dry and you will be far less likely to crack it as you remove the excess wood.

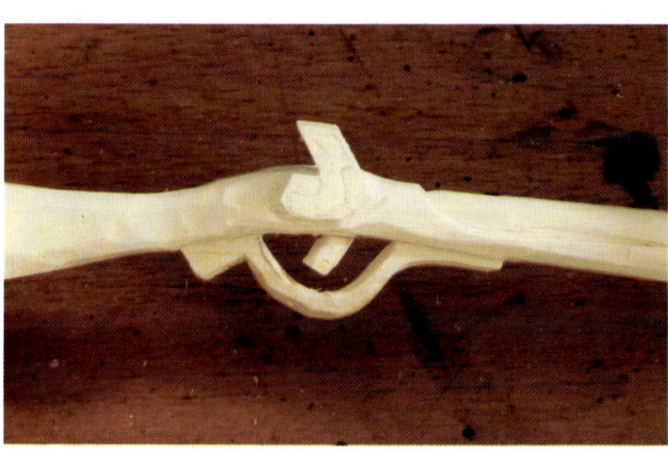

The completed trigger guard and trigger.

The mountain man and his rifle are ready for painting.

# Painting the Mountain Man

We're going to use Americana Acrylic Paints by Deco Art in a variety of colors which will be named as they are used. The brushes we'll use will vary in size from 00000 to a #5. I use a plastic bubble palette and a glue dispenser to mix my paints. The glue dispenser is ideal for transferring water to create the acryllic paint and water mixture. Most of the washes I use will start with a small amount of paint in the bottom of one of the bubbles in the palette. I will fill that bubble with water and mix the paint and water together using the brush. Experiment with the mixture until you achieve a consistency that you prefer.

Begin by painting the mountain man's buckskin shirt with DA93 Raw Sienna.

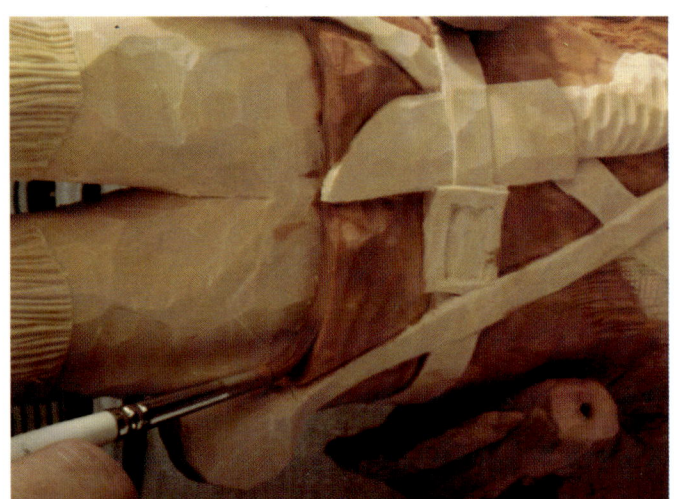

Don't forget to paint the undercut at the bottom of the shirt.

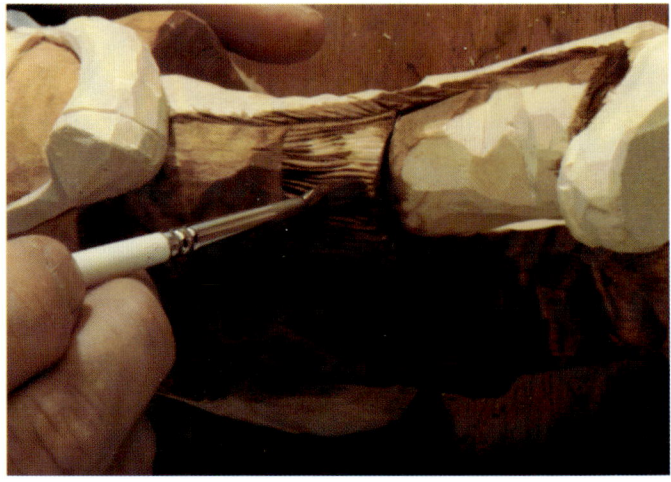

Use DA64 Burnt Umber to paint the pants.

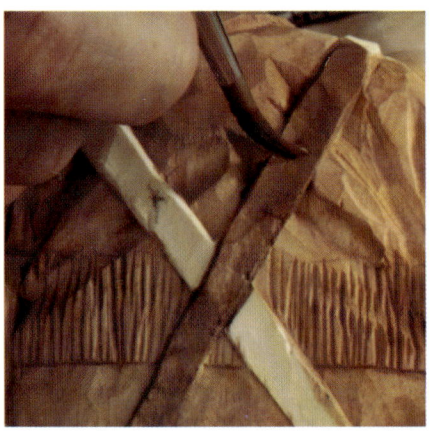

Paint the powder horn and the straps with this Burnt Umber wash.

While the body is drying, switch to the head and paint the flesh with DA102 Medium Flesh. Also use this color to paint the feet of the road kill animal cap. Once the face is painted, I use DA137 Shading Flesh to add a darker value to the flesh tone. I used a technique called wet-on-wet; that is, while the Medium Flesh was still wet on the face I applied Shading Flesh around the perimeter of the face—around the eyes, the smile lines, the nostrils, and under the lower lip.

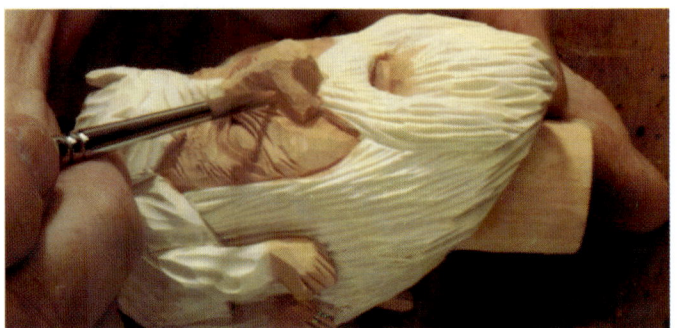

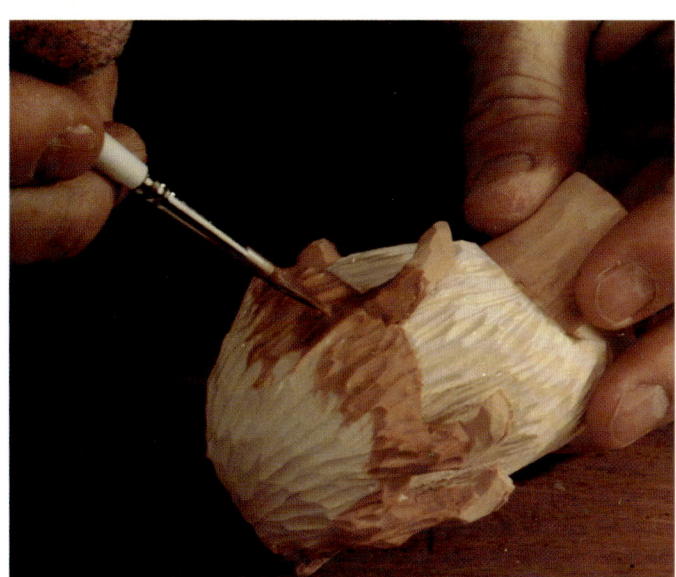

While we're on the head, let's use DA93, Raw Sienna, to paint the fur of the cap.

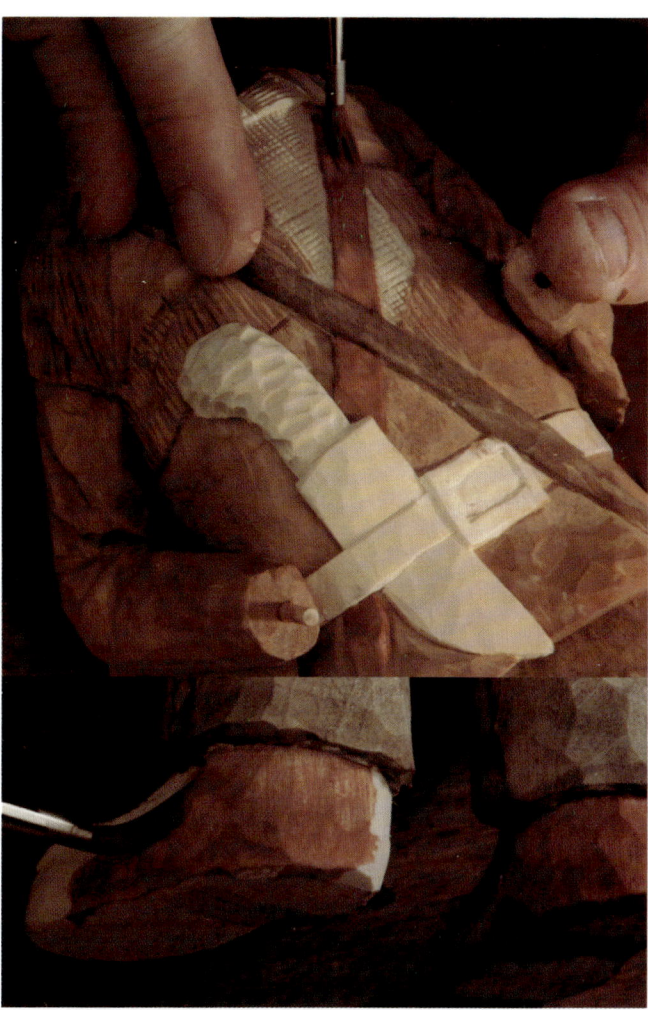

While the head is drying, use DA63 Burnt Sienna to paint the possibles bag and strap. Also use the Burnt Sienna to paint the lower portion of the moccasins below the seam line.

Use the DA64 Burnt Umber wash to paint the mountain man's hair, including the eyebrows.

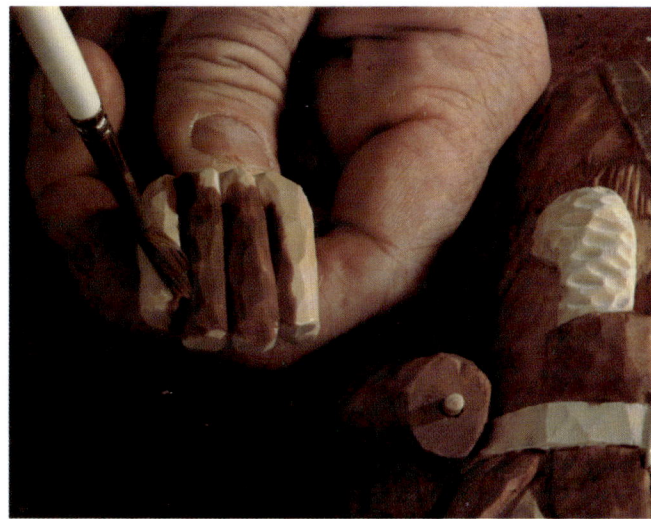

Use DA114 Light Cinnamon to paint the knife scabbard and the gloves.

51

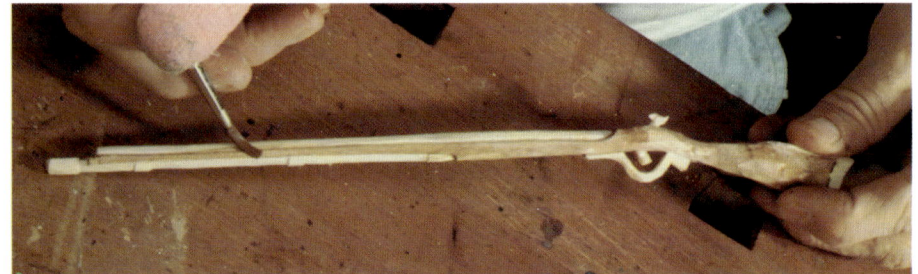

While the hands, head, and body are drying, paint the wood portion of the rifle with the DA64 Burnt Umber wash.

Paint the ramrod using DA63 Burnt Sienna.

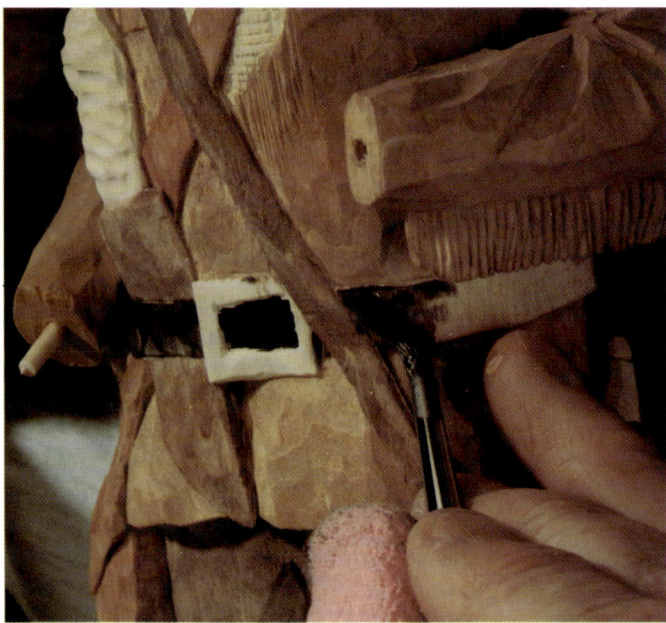

Use DA155 Soft Black to paint the belt ...

the gun barrel...

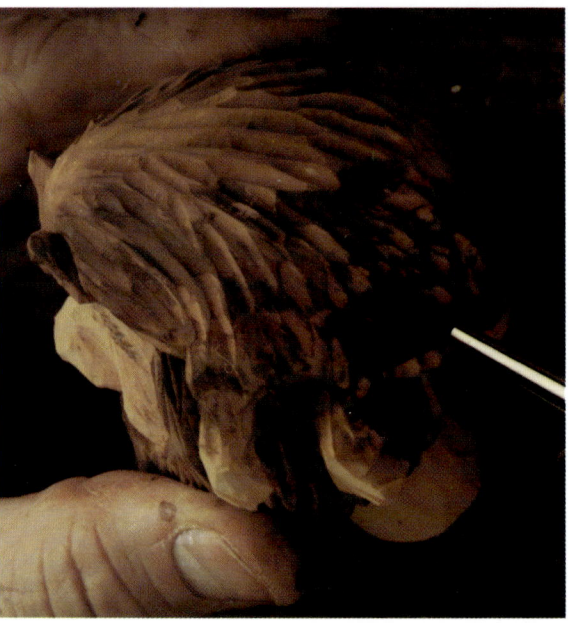

and to dry brush along the fur of the road kill cap. The dry brushing technique is one in which you load your brush with paint and, brushing across an absorbent paper, attempt to dry the brush, leaving only a little of this paint still in the fibers. When the brush is nearly dry, apply what little paint is left on the surface to be painted.

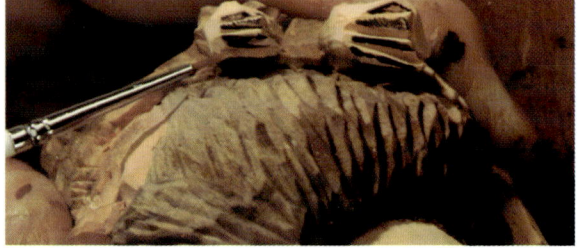

Use a small brush and some DA155 Soft Black straight from the tube to paint the toenails on the road kill's feet.

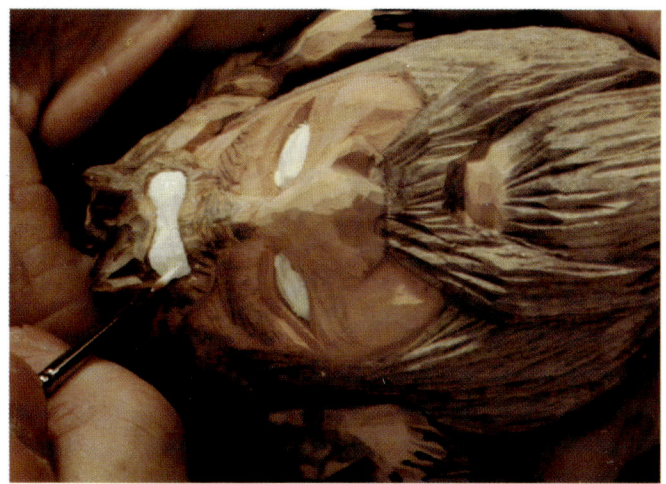

Using DA164 Light Buttermilk undiluted, paint the eyeballs on both the mountain man and his cap.

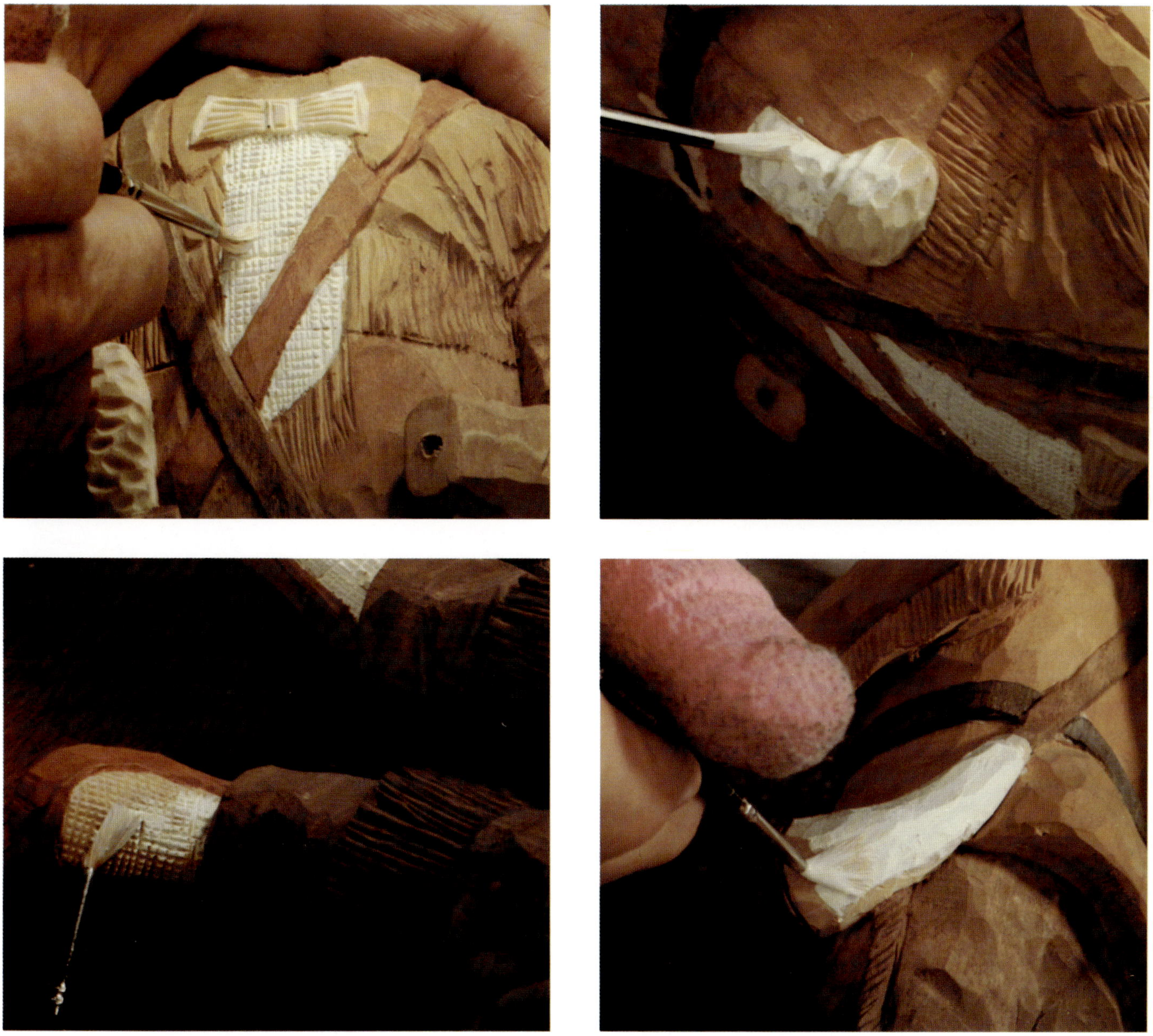

Paint the beadwork along the breast plate, the top of the moccasins, the knife handle, and the powder horn with undiluted DA164 Light Buttermilk.

Paint the iris on the eye using straight DA105 Blue-Grey Mist. Do not mix this paint with water for this job.

Using undiluted DA155 Soft Black, paint the pupils on the mountain man and his cap.

Add a dot of DA1 Titanium White to indicate light reflecting off the eyeballs.

Dry brush DA155 Soft Black wash onto the knife handle and the powder horn.

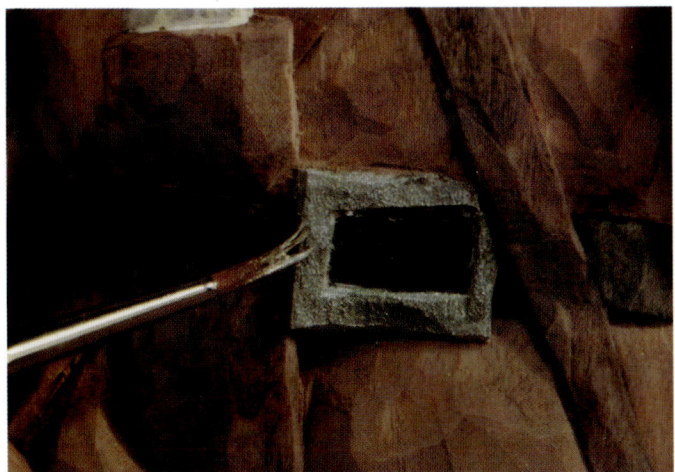

Take Shimmering Silver and paint the belt buckle...

the loading end of the powder horn ...

the hammer, the trigger, and the trigger guard.

Use Bronze to paint the ramrod holders...

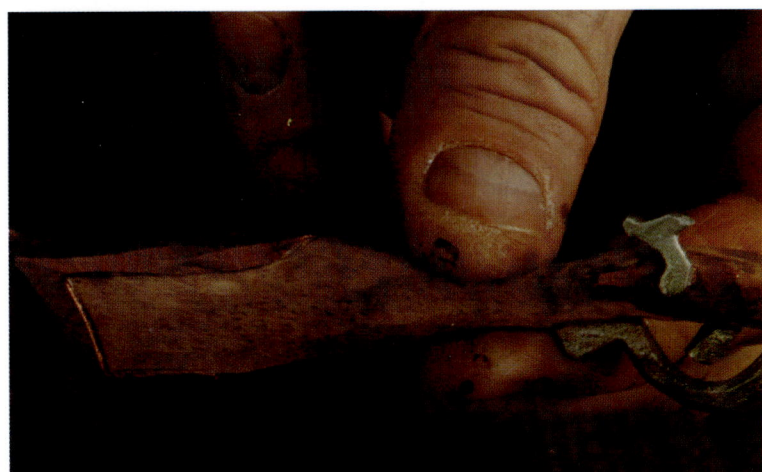

the scratch guard plate (around the hammer), and the butt plate of the gun stock.

Use DA1 Titanium White undiluted and dry brush the beard, mustache, and hair.

To finish up the coloration on the head, use an orange-red chalk and a short, stiff bristled brush and apply red to the cheeks, the tip of the nose, and the lips. This color is applied in much the same fashion as a woman would apply makeup.

Using DA44 Desert Turquoise, DA10 Cadmium Yellow, and DA20 Calico Red straight from the tube, paint some of the beadwork on the breastplate and the moccasins. Begin with Calico Red.

Surround the red with Cadmium Yellow. Complete the design by applying Desert Turquoise around the yellow.

Paint a different beadwork design onto the moccasin.

Finally, we will paint the reeds on the breastplate using Titanium White and Calico Red.

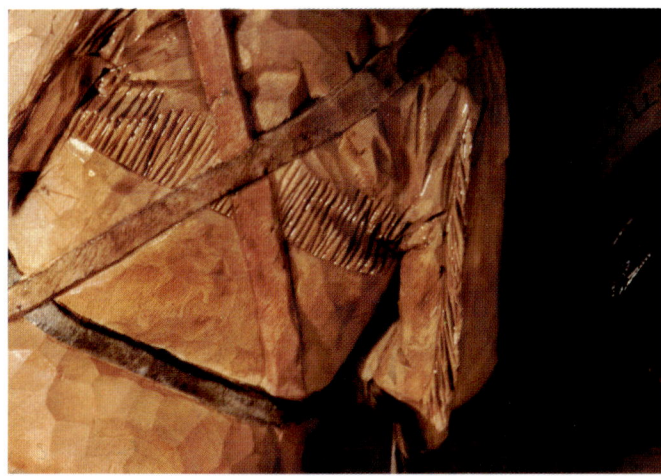

Seal all of the pieces with DS14 Matte Varnish. Once sealed, apply an antiquing mixture to the figure to complete the mountain man. Use a mixture of 4 parts Watco Satin Finishing Wax Natural and 1 part Watco Satin Finishing Wax Dark to create the antiquing solution. Darkness or lightness can be controlled by changing the mix, adding either more dark or clear wax to the mixture.

Place the rifle into the hands and carefully slide the hands over the dowels in the forearms.

After allowing the antiquing mixture to dry, use a horsehair shoe brush (or a power rotary brush of similar material, usable with a Foredom or Dremel power tool) and buff the waxed figure to a light-sheen.

The rifle and hands in place. This mountain man is complete.

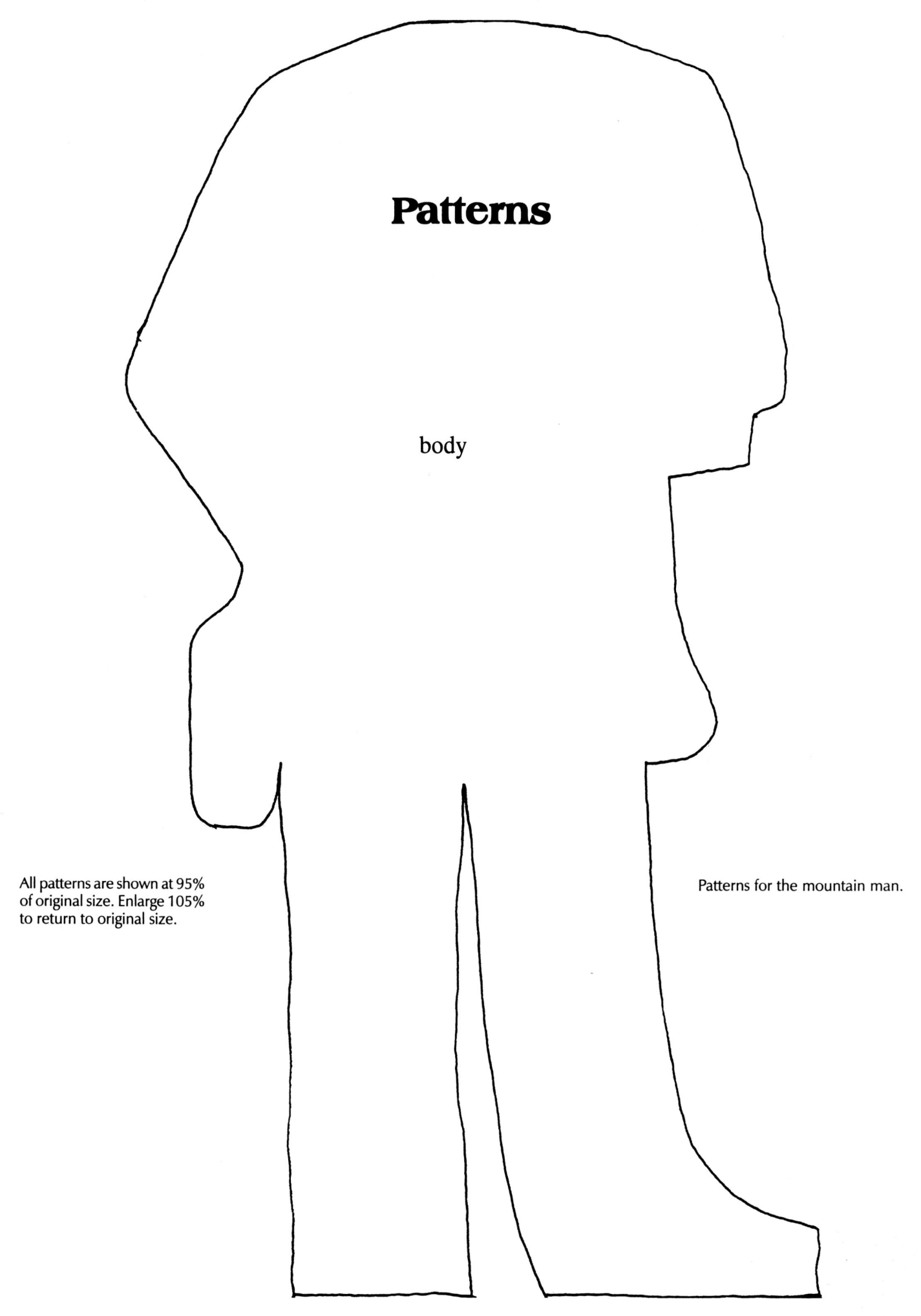

# Patterns

body

All patterns are shown at 95% of original size. Enlarge 105% to return to original size.

Patterns for the mountain man.

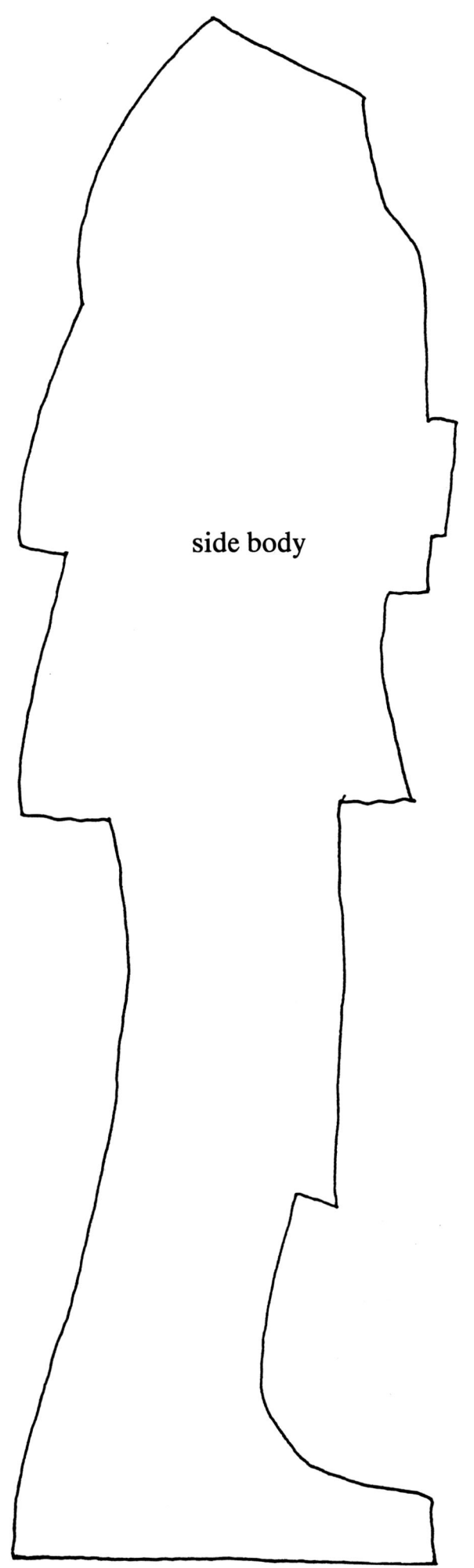
side body

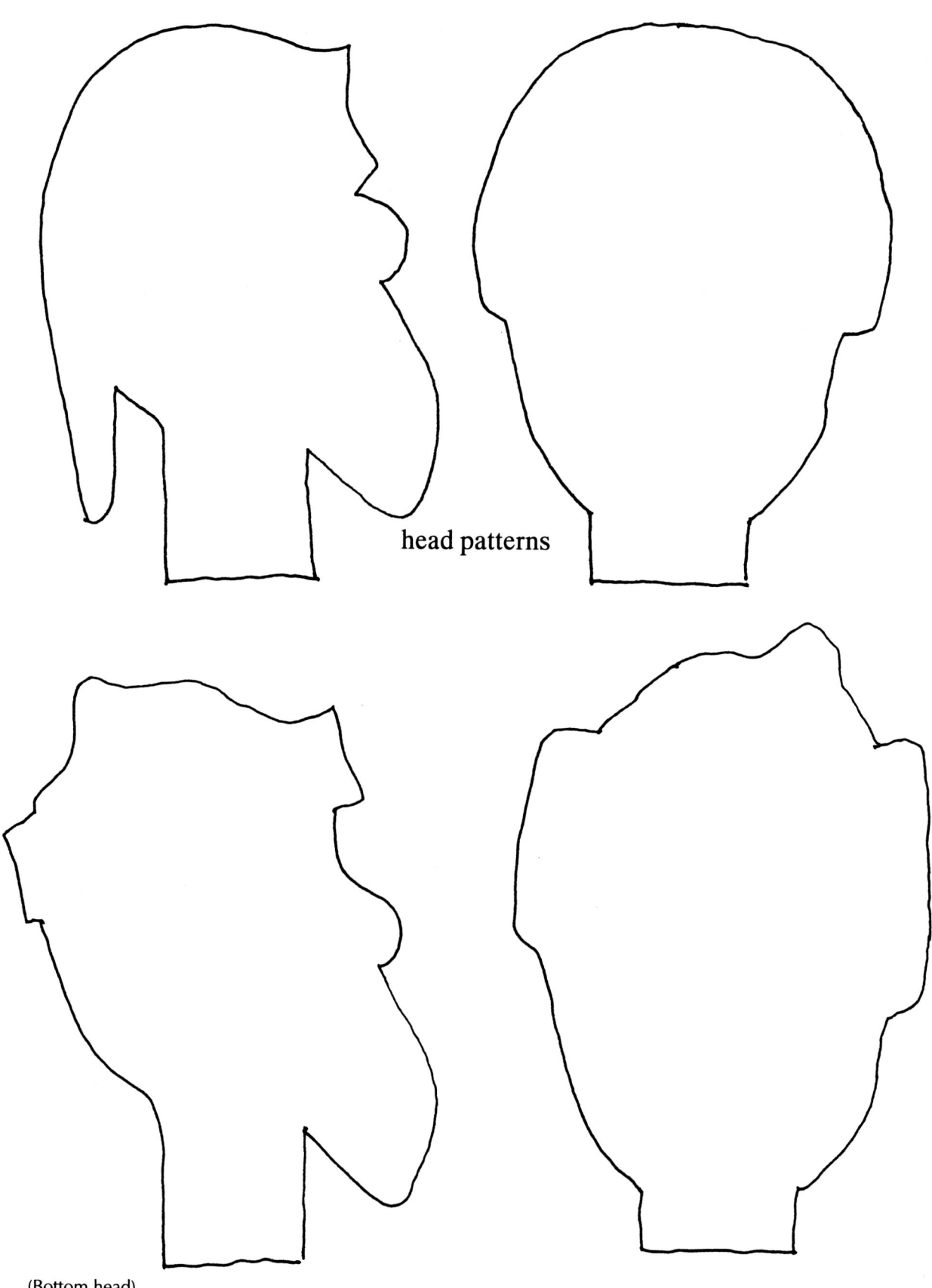

head patterns

(Bottom head)

An alternative head pattern; the mountain man wearing a Russian hat.

60

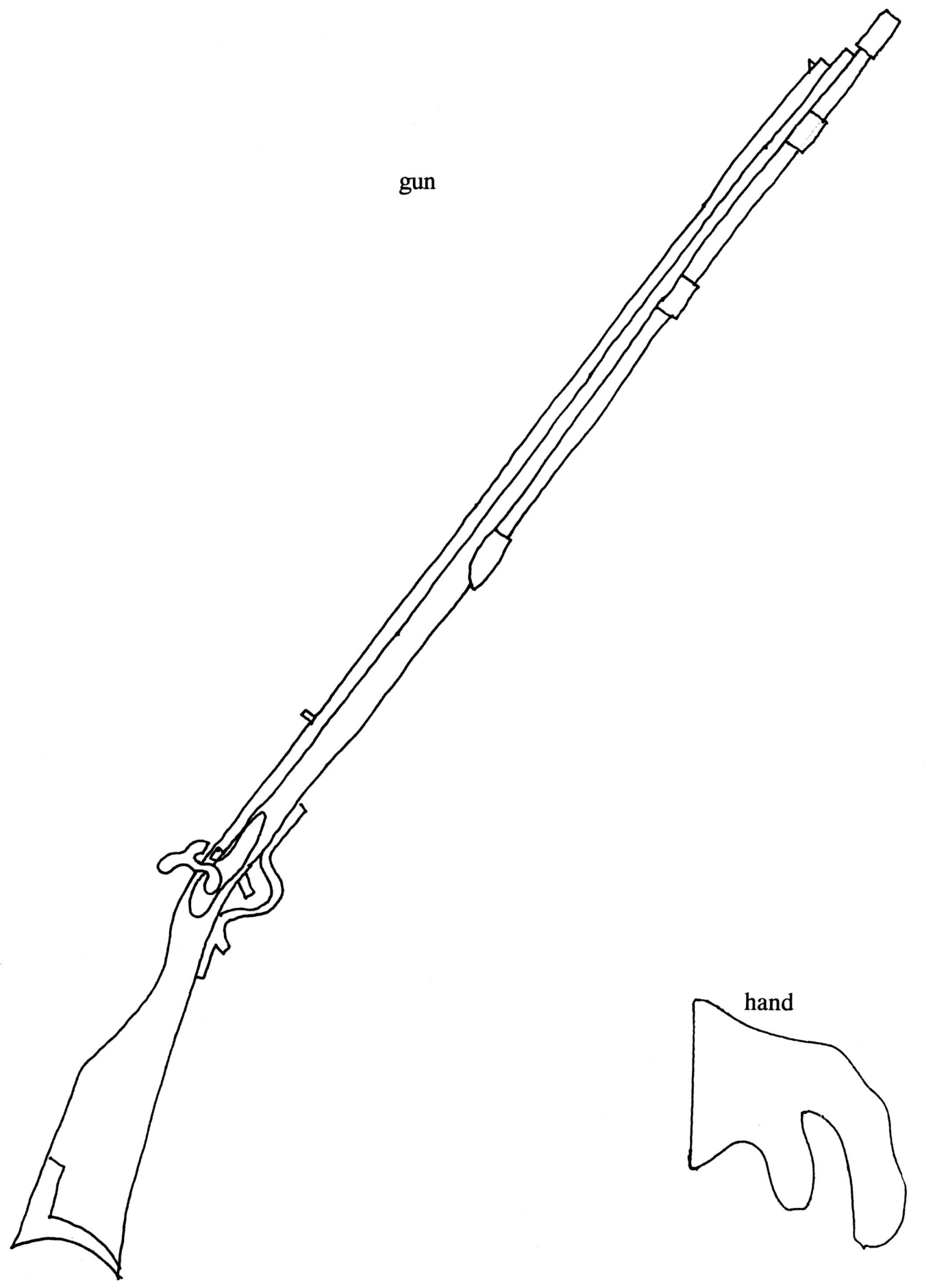

# Gallery

63

Here are two variations of the mountain man's head. Note the front leg on the skunk has been broken. Rather than gluing it back on, I have carved the stump of the bone sticking out.